"Before Susie Larson writes anointed, life-changing, Scripture-soaked words like the ones you'll read in this book, she lives and breathes them onto the pages of her life and into the hearts of those around her. I have been one of the blessed recipients of her words, wisdom, and brazen faith, and my life will never be the same because of Susie's prayers over me. And now, neither will yours! Drawing from the riches of God's Word and the power of His Spirit, Susie will empower and equip you to rise up and boldly claim what is yours in Christ through powerful prayers that move the heart of God!"

—Renee Swope, Word-Lover, Grace-Needer,
and Bestselling Author of *A Confident Heart*

"If you long for a more intimate relationship with God, this book will be a gift to your soul. If you have ever wondered if your life matters to God, Susie answers with a resounding yes!"

—Sheila Walsh, Bestselling Author and Bible Teacher

"To be sure, Satan does not want the lost saved. Even more than that, he trembles in fear that the saved will discover who they are in Christ. I suspect the enemy of our souls will do all he can to keep believers away from this excellent book. Susie Larson has a word for you—a wonderful word of strength, hope, and an empowered prayer life."

—Dr. Mark Rutland, *New York Times* Bestselling Author

"*Your Powerful Prayers* truly is powerful! Susie Larson does more than simply talk about prayer. She teaches us how to pray and reveals the miraculous ways God answers our prayers. Deep biblical truths and meaningful stories are woven throughout this life-changing resource. You'll write 'Yes!' across every page. I did!"

—Liz Curtis Higgs, Bestselling Author of *Bad Girls of the Bible*

"If you read only one book this year, make it this one! Susie Larson has poured her passion, her strong commitment to God's truth, and her unquenchable belief in the strength of prayer into this remarkable resource. Apply the principles in this book and you'll discover how to listen to God's voice through Scripture and how to pray God's Word. I highly recommend it for personal and for small group study. *Your Powerful Prayers* will transform the way you talk to God."

—Carol Kent, Speaker and Author of *When I Lay My Isaac Down*

"I read this book early in the morning when the clutter of distraction was yet to invade my head and heart. Each page reinforced something I've known about the author. Susie is a good friend—approachable and authentic, encouraging and empathetic, faithful and fun. But most of all, she is the kind of friend who doesn't disguise her friendship with Jesus. This book lacks camouflage and costumes, makeup and masks. It's clear and concise, and I found myself thinking about it the rest of the day."

—Jon Weece, Author and Lead Follower at Southland Christian Church, Kentucky

Your
Powerful
Prayers

Books by Susie Larson

Your Powerful Prayers

Reaching *the* Heart
of God *With a* Bold
and Humble Faith

SUSIE LARSON

BETHANYHOUSE
a division of Baker Publishing Group
Minneapolis, Minnesota

Published by Bethany House Publishers
11400 Hampshire Avenue South
Bloomington, Minnesota 55438
www.bethanyhouse.com

Bethany House Publishers is a division of
Baker Publishing Group, Grand Rapids, Michigan

Printed in the United States of America

Library of Congress Control Number: 2016931191

ISBN 978-0-7642-1332-8

Unless otherwise indicated, Scripture quotations are from the Holy Bible, New International Version®. NIV®. Copyright © 1973, 1978, 1984, 2011 by Biblica, Inc.™ Used by permission of Zondervan. All rights reserved worldwide. www.zondervan.com

Scripture quotations labeled AMP are from the Amplified® Bible, copyright © 2015 by The Lockman Foundation. Used by permission. (www.Lockman.org)

Scripture quotations labeled ESV are from The Holy Bible, English Standard Version® (ESV®), copyright © 2001 by Crossway, a publishing ministry of Good News Publishers. Used by permission. All rights reserved. ESV Text Edition: 2011

Scripture quotations labeled The Message are from THE MESSAGE. Copyright © by Eugene H. Peterson 1993, 1994, 1995, 1996, 2000, 2001, 2002. Used by permission of NavPress. All rights reserved. Represented by Tyndale House Publishers, Inc.

Scripture quotations labeled NKJV are from the New King James Version®. Copyright © 1982 by Thomas Nelson, Inc. Used by permission. All rights reserved.

Scripture quotations labeled NLT are from the Holy Bible, New Living Translation, copyright © 1996, 2004, 2015 by Tyndale House Foundation. Used by permission of Tyndale House Publishers, Inc., Carol Stream, Illinois 60188. All rights reserved.

Scripture quotations labeled TLB are from The Living Bible, copyright © 1971. Used by permission of Tyndale House Publishers, Inc., Carol Stream, Illinois 60188. All rights reserved.

Scripture quotations labeled The Voice are from The Voice™. Copyright © 2008 by Ecclesia Bible Society. Used by permission. All rights reserved.

Cover design by Faceout Studio, Emily Weigel
Interior artwork by Andy McGuire

Author is represented by The Steve Laube Agency

16   17   18   19   20   21   22   7   6   5   4   3   2   1

To my youngest son, Jordan
I watched you walk through the valley of the shadow
with honor, humility, and conviction. You're an amazing
young man. Dad and I are so blessed to call you our son.

To the Nazarene
You became sin, though You never once sinned,
that we might become the righteousness of God.

Jesus, I ask You to pour out Your spirit
on the precious souls who pick up this book.

May You do a wonder-working miracle in their lives.
Empower their prayers. Ignite their faith.
And change the world through them.
In Jesus' name, I pray, Amen.

Contents

Foreword

The Spirit of God is moving.

Last year I, too, wrote a book on prayer. As did several other Christian authors. Susie then told me she also was finishing a book on prayer. At first I thought I had made a mistake; apparently I had jumped on some bandwagon I wasn't even aware of. But then I saw the signs for what they really were—proof that the Spirit of God is moving. God is raising up His people to pray. I think He knows we are facing hard times, and like a good Father He wants to equip us.

But as I began talking about prayer on radio shows and blogs, I discovered that God's dear people had some real misunderstandings about prayer, and a good deal of disappointment. Mostly disappointment. Many had, in fact, given up on prayer altogether, which is like a soldier laying down his weapons in the midst of a firefight. Giving up on prayer at this moment is not a wise thing to do!

But I understand the disappointment. I think we made an assumption that wound up hurting us. We thought prayer was simply asking God to do something, and then waiting to see if He did it. When it seemed that God ignored our prayers, we were hurt. And gave up.

But notice how the people who walked closest to Jesus saw it: They watched the prayer life of their Master, and their reaction was, "Teach us to pray" (Luke 11:1). *Teach us* to pray! In other words, they realized prayer is something to be learned, something we need some coaching in. Prayer is, in fact, far more like learning to drive or getting married or becoming a parent than like sneezing. It isn't quick and easy; it is something you grow into, something you mature in and get better at over time. Just like the young couple who at first thought, *All a marriage needs is love*, the disciples discovered they had a lot to learn in order to pray effectively. And the sooner they got to it the better things were going to go.

Now *that* is a hopeful view of prayer.

Because we *can* learn and grow, and we *do* get the hang of it, and then—much to our joy—we begin to see far more results in our prayers. Isn't that why we pray—to see things change?

That is why you will love this book. Susie has learned in the best school of all—the school of hard knocks—just what powerful prayer looks like and how to stick with it. And she has a lot to say to us. Susie is among my favorite radio hosts because she is real and she loves God and she *gets it*. This is a woman with a real prayer life. She's talking about things she has learned from the Master.

And that is why she can say your prayers will become powerful, too. They will. And the world will never be the same.

John Eldredge

Introduction

Some things may be neglected with but little loss to the spiritual life, but to neglect communion with God is to hurt ourselves where we cannot afford it.

A.W. Tozer, *Tozer for the Christian Leader*

The sense of God's presence *can* become the unwavering possession of our souls.

F. B. Meyer, *Streams in the Desert*

And so I walk in the LORD's presence as I live here on earth!

Psalm 116:9 NLT

I have a distinct nighttime memory of me as a little girl, curled up in a ball on my bed, afraid to move an inch. I pull the covers up over my head and whisper, "Dear God, be my shield of protection." I have no idea God breathed those very words on the pages of Scripture. I don't know much about God at all at this point except that He is real. And so I pray.

13

Every night, with my knees tucked close to my heart, I nestle under my blanket and ask God to cover me. I utter the prayer of a little girl who has been hurt at the hands of teenage boys. Though I come from a wonderful family, fear fastened itself to my soul, which affected my view of the world and of God. My prayers as a young girl are born out of insecurity, an aching soul, and a desperate need for someone stronger than I am to help me.

This is my perspective:

- Mean and hurtful people walk the earth.
- I'm small and have no voice.
- God is big and *out there* somewhere.
- I'm vulnerable.
- I pray He'll come through for me.

Like flicking a feather into the air and hoping it catches flight, I toss my prayers in the air in hopes they'll somehow reach the ears of God.

In eighth grade I come to know Jesus as my Savior. Even though I understand that I am saved, I don't at all grasp that *I am loved*. Most of my prayers—and my everyday choices, for that matter—are born out of a straining, striving, hope-I-can-jump-high-enough-for-God-to-bless-me kind of mind-set.

It isn't even until I've been married for several years that I realize I still curl into a little ball at night. Which leaves the rest of our king-sized bed to my husband. I have all this space available to me, yet fear pulls me to its corner. By then I considered myself a pretty serious follower of Christ. But my choices and my prayers still bear the signs of someone not quite convinced that she is the object of God's profound delight and lavish love.

Imagine my amazement when, later on in life, I stumbled onto truths and verses like these:

- God is my shield of protection: *"Every word of God is flawless; he is a shield to those who take refuge in him"* (Proverbs 30:5).

- My cry reaches His ears: *"In my distress I called to the* LORD; *I cried to my God for help. From his temple he heard my voice; my cry came before him, into his ears"* (Psalm 18:6).

- He knows my name and will come for me: *"Don't be afraid, I've redeemed you. I've called your name. You're mine. When you're in over your head, I'll be there with you. When you're in rough waters, you will not go down. When you're between a rock and a hard place, it won't be a dead end—Because I am God, your personal God, The Holy of Israel, your Savior"* (Isaiah 43:1–3 THE MESSAGE).

- I have authority: *"Look, I have given you authority over all the power of the enemy, and you can walk among snakes and scorpions and crush them. Nothing will injure you"* (Luke 10:19 NLT).

- His love (not my striving) is what fills me up to overflowing: *"May you experience the love of Christ, though it is too great to understand fully. Then you will be made complete with all the fullness of life and power that comes from God"* (Ephesians 3:19 NLT).

- Things change when I pray: *"The earnest prayer of a righteous person has great power and produces wonderful results"* (James 5:16 NLT).

Looking back over the years, I've noticed that my personal prayer life evolved this way:

- Vulnerable young girl: *Prayers of protection*
- Young woman, searching heart: *Prayers for identity, confidence, and to know God more*

15

- A woman in crisis: *Prayers of bulldog faith based on the power of God's promises and the treasure of His presence*
- A woman on a mission: *Audacious prayers born from the knowledge that I'm loved, called, equipped, and sent*

Jesus has never failed me. He's invited me—one baby step at a time—to stretch out and explore the depths and the power of fellowship with Him. He wants me to be comfortable with, yet at the same time *undone by*, His great love for me. I'm learning how to accept His profound and lavish acceptance of me.

What does God's love and acceptance of us have to do with prayer?

Everything.

Think about your own journey. You too have your own bruises and battle wounds. Your experiences have no doubt shaped your view of God. Maybe you've found that when you pray, some things change, but others, not so much. Maybe you wonder if His promises are true *for you*.

Can I tell you, friend? They are! His promises are true for you. He invites you to know Him more intimately, to walk with Him more profoundly, and to trust in His Word more confidently.

Do you long for your whole soul to be filled with the fullness of God so that your life spills with grace, insight, and power? You can. Jesus says so. Here's the answer:

Get to know this love.

Re-read this powerful verse: *"May you experience the love of Christ, though it is too great to understand fully. Then you will be made complete with all the fullness of life and power that comes from God"* (Ephesians 3:19 NLT).

If we want to be powerful in prayer, we must spend our lives learning to accept and embrace how fiercely God loves us. We must continually stand in awe of the fact that Jesus defeated death and sin *for us*. And then from there, live our whole lives in response to what Jesus has already accomplished for us. This is what it means to stop our striving and to know that He is God (Psalm 46:10).

The more we pursue Jesus, the more we understand how relentlessly He *pursues us*. Jesus wants to talk with us. He wants to hear what we have to say. He has power to establish us, things to teach us, direction to give us. We need Him. And He deeply wants us near Him.

If we live our lives and we approach our prayers as though we're trying hard to jump high enough to reach the sky, we'll only wear ourselves out. We'll pray weak prayers, and we'll never fully experience what God has made available to us.

> *If we want to be powerful in prayer, we must spend our lives learning to accept and embrace how fiercely God loves us.*

The truth is, love came down and rescued us. Jesus came to us. He died for us. He defeated the powers that oppose us. And now He sits at the right hand of the Father, praying for us. Imagine!

We have access to the throne room of heaven because of Jesus. We get to enjoy His presence. We get to draw on His resources. We get to trust in His love. We get to count on His promises. And we are invited to pray in agreement with the prayers He's already praying for us. Read Eugene Peterson's beautiful paraphrase of Romans 5:1–2 in THE MESSAGE:

> By entering through faith into what God has always wanted to do for us—set us right with him, make us fit for him—we have it all together with God because of our Master Jesus. And that's not all: We throw open our doors to God and discover at the same moment that he has already thrown open his door to us. We find ourselves standing where we always hoped we might stand—out in the wide open spaces of God's grace and glory, standing tall and shouting our praise.

You probably already know this, but it bears repeating: The Word of God and your prayer life are your lifelines. If you pray without regularly reading the Word, you'll be like a ship without a sail. You'll wander wherever the winds take you. If you read the Word without engaging in prayer, you'll be like a sail without a ship. The wind may fill your sail, but you'll never get anywhere.

Jesus is committed to getting you safely home. And to the extent that you read His Word, you will recognize His truth. To the extent that you trust His love, you will be powerful in prayer. And, the more you grasp God's great heart for you, you will embrace His heart for the greater kingdom story He's writing on the earth today.

Prayer not only invites Jesus' involvement in our everyday affairs—prayer changes us. Prayer links us in intimate fellowship with the God of heaven who sings beautiful songs over us, who loves us, and who will never—no, never—forsake us.

Jesus wants to teach us things we do not know. He wants to open our eyes to things we could never perceive on our own. And *He wants to hear from us.* He wants us to be free to express what's on our hearts. He wants to use us to impact the world today. He guards, He guides, He corrects, He protects, and He provides. He invites us into His inner courts because we belong to Him.

And though He answers prayers, grants us some of the deepest desires of our hearts, and tends to the things that concern us, Jesus Himself is our greatest treasure. Any gift from His hand pales in comparison to the treasure of knowing His heart.

Andrew Murray wrote:

When the name of Jesus has become the power that rules my life, power in prayer with God will be evident as well. Everything depends on the name; the power it has *on* my life is the power it will have *in* my prayers.[1]

Jesus isn't a means to an end. He's the beginning and the end. He's not at our beck and call. We're the ones who wait on Him. He's not biding His time until we give Him something to do; we receive our marching orders from Him.

And yet. *And yet*, He listens to us. He's moved by our heart's cry. He empowers our obedience. He strengthens our soul. He moves when we pray. And He transforms us as we go. The power in our prayers is directly connected to God's power in our lives.

So the question of the day is this: How surrendered are we willing to be? How much access will we give Him to our story? Will we trust Him? Do we believe that He is good and mighty and true?

We can pray as ones who are not only spoken for by God Himself, but as ones who have His Spirit alive in us, His promises offered to us, and His presence with us, every step of the way. Prayer links us in fellowship with the star-breathing God. Prayer strengthens our faith, encourages our hearts, changes our circumstances and/or perspective, and impacts our story as we dialogue with God about what we see in the world.

One last thought I want to leave you with before we dig into this book study. The place of power, the sweet spot in our faith walk, is that place where joy and faith collide. Jesus invites us to a hilarious-dancing-leaping kind of joy—a joy that invites us

The power in your prayers is directly connected to God's power in your life.

to relish our food, enjoy our loved ones, stand in awe of a sunset, and embrace His goodness because every good gift comes from His hand.

This kind of joy—the joy of the Lord Himself—is our strength. It's a discipline and a fruit. When we choose joy and taste and see that God is good (even when He's not giving us what we want at the moment), we come to enjoy the joy of the Lord.

Then there's tenacious faith. We cannot please God without faith. Faith is our substance, our spiritual traction; it's evidence of our trust in a faithful God.

Many Christians live with little spiritual traction, never fully enjoying the joy of the Lord and never fully embracing a fierce faith that engages God and His promises. Picture these two things—hilarious joy and fierce faith—standing miles apart. Many Christians live in that dull land in between: underwhelmed, uninspired, under-joyed, and under-faithed.

But imagine bringing the two together, side by side, as if no more space existed between these two forces. Imagine if these two invitations—hilarious joy and fierce faith—were continually and consistently juxtaposed in your life. Imagine if winsome joy marked your life in every way, every day. Imagine learning to enjoy every good thing in your life as a gift from God and thus cultivating a perpetual heart of gratitude and thanksgiving. And imagine having such a fierce faith that you know how to pray, and things change when you pray. Imagine having a firmer grip on His promises.

Fierce faith. Hilarious joy. Think it's not possible? It is.

And it's the only way to live.

Don't you want to experience God's presence and power in your life in ever-increasing measures? Don't you want your capacity for His love, your understanding of His grace, and your grasp of His promises to increase with each passing day? I do too.

I don't know how you'd describe your own prayer life, but my prayer for you is that no matter where you find yourself, you'll find God right in your midst, and your prayer life growing by leaps and bounds.

In the chapters ahead, we'll explore what it means to be heirs of God. We'll learn how to have a firmer grasp of who we are, because we are in Christ. We'll read about the power of prayer, and then pray powerful prayers every single day.

20

Lord willing, by the time you're done with this book, you will have bulldog faith, tenacious hope, and a more profound sense of your unchangeable identity in Christ. You'll be like a skilled Olympic athlete, conditioned to stand in faith, trained to stand in battle, and prepared to pray prayers that move God's heart in a way that changes the world. I'm so very grateful to be on this journey with you. I'll be praying for you every single day.

In Christ Jesus,
Susie Larson

God, Your Fortress

I love you, LORD; you are my strength.
The LORD is my rock, my fortress, and my savior;
my God is my rock, in whom I find protection.
He is my shield, the power that saves me, and my place
    of safety.

Psalm 18:1–2 NLT

1

Dare to Pray Like You're Loved

You're Secure in Jesus

God is still pursuing you *after* you've placed your faith in Him—
not to burden you with more tasks on the to-do list or to whip
you into shape, but to love you. He pursues you with an intensity
that can breathe life into you.

Jud Wilhite, Pursued

But blessed is the one who trusts in the Lord, whose confidence
is in him. They will be like a tree planted by the water that sends
out its roots by the stream. It does not fear when heat comes; its
leaves are always green. It has no worries in a year of drought
and never fails to bear fruit.

Jeremiah 17:7–8

As a young mom, I remember lying facedown on the floor, face
buried in the carpet, crying my eyes out. I'd been betrayed and
rejected by friends. Their treatment of me reflected how I really

felt about myself. I couldn't get out from under the weight of the condemnation and rejection that threatened to suffocate me. I cried out to God and begged Him to help me catch my breath, when suddenly a peace washed over me.

I sensed Him right there with me, as if He sat on the floor next to me with His strong and tender hand on my back. I heard the whisper in my heart, "I am here for you. . . . You don't have to do this alone. I know rejection. I know the twisting, gripping pain that breaks your heart and makes your skin hurt. I understand it well. But it's time to get up now. *I* love you. *I* accept you. And, you have things to do in this life. For starters, you are going to pray for your accusers."[1]

I sat up, squeezed the last drops of tears from my eyes, and wiped away the wetness from my cheeks. I looked out the window and felt utterly grateful for the gift of prayer; amazed that God invites me into a two-way conversation. I heard (though not audibly) the voice of my Savior. And His words got me up off the floor again.

Read these precious and profound words from A.W. Tozer:

> How unutterably sweet is the knowledge that our Heavenly Father knows us completely. No talebearer can inform on us, no enemy can make an accusation stick; no forgotten skeleton can come tumbling out of some hidden closet to abash us and expose our past; no unsuspected weakness in our characters can come to light to turn God away from us, since He knew us utterly before we knew Him and called us to Himself in the full knowledge of everything that was against us. . . . Our Father in heaven knows our frame and remembers that we are dust. He knew our inborn treachery, and for His own sake engaged to save us (Isa. 48:8–11). His only begotten Son, when He walked among us, felt our pains in their naked intensity of anguish. His knowledge of our afflictions and adversities is more than theoretic; it is personal, warm, and compassionate. Whatever may befall us, God knows and cares as no one else can.[2]

Trust His Love

Something gets healed in us when we trust God's love. Something comes alive in us when—amidst the pain we endure—we still believe that *He is good*. Something is mobilized in us when we understand that He wired us to partner with Him in a way that fits who we are.

Jesus didn't save us so He can have millions of slaves at His service, all running hard in the same direction, looking exactly alike, all doing the same thing. If we are in Christ, we're no longer slaves. *We are sons and daughters*. He grants us an elevated status, even above the angels.

Still, how He engages with you may be different from how He engages with me. He's the same God, but He's made us each wonderfully unique. And He invites us to know Him intimately and profoundly. He wants us to enjoy Him, because He truly enjoys us.

Consider this in human terms. My three sons couldn't be more different from each other. And I love it that way. I see parts of my image in them. I see parts of my husband, Kevin, in them too. And I see how and why God wired them each with their own convictions for a distinct purpose. I love that they're different. I love how they're different. And I love them because they're mine.

I also see the lies they picked up when life let them down.

And so I pray.

I pray like there's a God in heaven who hears me when I pray and who answers me when I call on Him. You know why? Because there *is* a God in heaven who hears me when I pray and who answers me when I call on Him.

Something comes alive in us when we believe that God is good.

He's committed to you. He cares about your story. He likes how He made you. He'll untangle your fears. He'll extract the lies embedded in your soul and impart truths that will set you free.

27

Though Jesus invites us to pray at all times, about everything, in every season, prayer isn't just a vehicle to get what we want from God. First and foremost, prayer connects us to the One who loves our soul. Prayer links us in fellowship with the Most High God. Prayer's primary purpose in our lives is that we might enjoy intimacy with our Creator and participate with His purposes here on earth.

Jennifer Kennedy Dean explains the purpose of prayer beautifully here:

> Prayer is the means by which you will be freed from your earthbound, timebound thinking to participate in eternity. True prayer releases His power so that His power can accomplish immeasurably more than we can ask or even imagine.[3]

Unfortunately, some folks will get to heaven and realize that though they were saved, they never understood or lived in true freedom. They lived in constant reaction to their issues and insecurities. They never shook free of the constant sins that plagued them. They lived far beneath their spiritual privilege because they never looked up and firmly grabbed hold of God's promises or His identity imparted to them.

The truth is, though God deeply loves these precious souls, they missed out on the adventure of partnering with God to see His purposes fulfilled on the earth in their lifetimes.

God invites us to a life marked by power and filled with conviction, one that abounds in love and pours out insight. As we walk with Him, talk with Him, read His Word, and trust His heart, we are changed from the inside out.

Secure in Him

Here's one thing I wish someone would have told me long ago: Though it takes time to mature as a Christian, our *status* is secure in Christ, no matter where we are on this faith journey. You can't rush maturity. But you don't have to wait to be powerful in prayer.

The minute you receive Christ, you become a new creation. You have the Holy Spirit actively at work within you. Scripture says that the same power that raised Christ from the dead is in you. In you![4]

What does it mean for followers of Christ, whether brand-new believers or seasoned Christians, to have the Spirit of the living God alive in our souls? Let's look at what Scripture says:

> His divine power has given us everything we need for a godly life through our knowledge of him who called us by his own glory and goodness. Through these he has given us his very great and precious promises, so that through them you may participate in the divine nature, having escaped the corruption in the world caused by evil desires.
>
> 2 Peter 1:3–4

I plan to unpack this passage more in-depth on the companion DVD study to this book, but for now, consider that God's divine power has given you *everything you need* for a godly life, which you will more easily access the more you get to know Him. He invites you into this back-and-forth dialogue and adventure of faith and obedience because of His own glory and goodness.

And because of His profound and passionate heart for you, He's given you these very great and precious promises. Why? So that you can participate in the *divine nature*, which means God Himself empowers you to live an otherworldly life, not bogged down by your "natural" circumstances!

Sure, we'll encounter trouble on this earth. Jesus said so. But as we lay hold of God's promises and walk in His power, His Spirit in us allows us to defy the gravity of sin and circumstance, and to pray as one who has been and will continue to be redeemed from this life on earth.

We can have as much of God as we want. What will we do with what God has made available to us during our lifetime?

And think about this: What we possess of Him here deeply impacts how our lives play out in eternity. One day we'll have to answer to Jesus for every opportunity, every gift, and every promise He's offered us. How will we respond? Will our life's work go up in smoke? Or will it echo into eternity?[5]

Do we call ourselves *believers* only because we trusted Christ for our salvation? Or do we actually believe that Jesus wants to hear from us? Do we believe with our whole heart that His promises are true for us? Do we believe that our ongoing conversations with God actually impact His influence in and through us? And are we willing to stake our lifestyle on the fact that whether or not we pray matters in the whole scheme of things?

Andrew Murray once asked, "Who could predict what blessing might come through those who agree to prove God's promises?"[6]

What if we just trusted that what Jesus said is true? What if we shifted the weight of our worries, our hopes, our dreams, and our burdens all onto Him, the one who keeps His promises? What if we walked through life with a contagious joy, a lighter burden, and a fiercer faith? What if our ongoing dialogue with the Almighty reflected a heart that fully trusts God's movement and mercy in our lives?

May it be said of us that we live like God's promises are true because we know in the depths of our souls that they really, truly are.

A Blessing for You

May you respond to the invitation to be much more with God than you've ever been before. May you take the next steps to trust Him with greater expectancy, and to call on Him with greater fervency, and to obey Him with greater expediency. Nothing on earth compares to intimately knowing the One who spoke the galaxies into existence. And He wants to hear from *you*.

Let's Pray . . .

Thank you, Lord, for Your great love. Thank you for wooing me, for pursuing me, and for chasing after me when I lose my way. Help me to see Your image imprinted on my heart. Open my eyes to the wonders of Your great love. Take me by the hand and lead me to a rock that is higher than I, so I can see what You see. I want to do what You'd do, say what You'd say, and pray what You'd pray if You were walking in my shoes today. Redeem my story so that my whole life reflects Your great love. I am Yours and You are mine. Your banner over me is love. Thank you, Lord.

Praying God's Word

Write out a personalized prayer and weave in the truths of the following Scripture. Make the declaration that no matter what you're facing right now, nothing can separate you from the love of God!

For I am convinced that neither death nor life, neither angels nor demons, neither the present nor the future, nor any powers, neither height nor depth, nor anything else in all creation, will be able to separate us from the love of God that is in Christ Jesus our Lord.

Romans 8:38–39

A POWERFUL WORD: *I Want More*

It is time to know what we want. It is time to stop chasing the temporary in place of the eternal. It is time to stop putting wages in our pockets only to have them exit through the holes. It is time to come back to God, beg Him for revival, and start moving forward into the most and best that can be ours.[7]

Personal Reflection

1. In what situations do you tend not to pray, but worry instead?

2. Is this a repeated pattern for you? Explain.

3. Honest answer here: How do you think God feels about you?

4. When in your life did God's love feel most tangible to you?

5. How often do you think about God's thoughts toward you?

6. Starting today, will you ask God to open your eyes and powerfully awaken your heart to His affection for you? I dare you!

7. How might your prayer life change as you recognize God's unfathomable love for you? Write down your best answer.

Group Reflection

1. We tend to pray about the same things over and over. Sometimes this is all about perseverance, yet other times our repetition reveals a certain unbelief and unwillingness to turn our cares over to God. What (if you don't mind sharing) are the things you pray most often about? Would you say it's perseverance or unbelief that's driving you?

2. Share about a time when you experienced a direct answer to prayer.

3. In what other areas of your life do you desire to see God move and influence the circumstances? Explain.

4. How often do you think about God's thoughts toward you?

5. Why do you suppose our prayer life is so impacted by our understanding of God's love for us?

6. In the days ahead, how would you like to see your prayer life grow?

7. When was the last time you sensed God's tangible love for you?

2

Dare to Pray for Perspective

You're Part of a Bigger Story

Sometimes God wraps His glory in hard circumstances or ugly obstacles or painful difficulties, and it just never occurs to us that within those life-shaking events is a fresh revelation from Him.

Anne Graham Lotz, *Expecting to See Jesus*

I waited patiently for the LORD to help me, and he turned to me and heard my cry. He lifted me out of the pit of despair, out of the mud and the mire. He set my feet on solid ground and steadied me as I walked along. He has given me a new song to sing, a hymn of praise to our God. Many will see what he has done and be amazed. They will put their trust in the LORD.

Psalm 40:1–3 NLT

Several years ago I walked through a significantly dark night of the soul. And while I'm not ready to share the details quite yet, I will say to you what my friend Jodi told me: "If the story is not good yet, it's because God is not done yet." If you're in a not-yet season, and if that season involves heartbreak or disappointment, it's especially important to keep perspective, to remember who you are, and to hang on to God's promises even when they don't feel true. What we say about our disappointments and what we *pray* about our disappointments deeply matters and reflects what we believe to be true about God and ourselves.

Someone once said that we're always close to a storm; either we're walking into a storm, enduring a storm, or coming out of a storm. While it's true that God gives us seasons of rest and peace (thank God for those!), life on earth can be hard, grueling, heartbreaking, and soul wrenching.

What are we to do with the life disappointments that pack a punch and leave us breathless? Do we stop praying altogether? Change our view of God? Turn our back on Him? Pray begging-pleading kinds of prayers? Or do we remember that we're heirs, and live accordingly?

We all sort through our losses and hardships in different ways. It's absolutely precious that God invites us to lament, to pour out our hearts to Him, and to grieve wholeheartedly, messy as it can be at times. And He never—not for a moment—looks away, rolls His eyes, or loves us less. Amazing, yes?

But I noticed for me that in the midst of my sadness and grief, certain questions stole my perspective instead of clarifying it; they took the wind out of my sails and pulled me backward instead of pushing me forward. Maybe you can relate:

- *HOW could this have happened, Lord? I did my part, didn't I?*
- *WHY did this happen, Lord? Why didn't You intervene?*

Though at the outset of loss or pain, our souls will instinctively cry out such questions. I knew for me, I needed to move on from this place and ask different questions, ones that compelled me to look up and remember that God is good, His promises are true, and He'll always make a way for me.

I'll share those questions in a bit, but first let's take a look at a woman who endured significant loss in her family. So much so, she felt sure that not only had God abandoned her, He'd actually stretched out His hand against her to destroy her. We can learn a lot from a woman who battled devastating, destructive disappointment.

In the book of Ruth we read about Naomi and her husband, Elimelech. Together they had two sons. They lived in Bethlehem. Until there was a famine in the land.

They lived in the center of God's will for them, until they were no longer getting what they wanted from God. Then they took matters into their own hands.

Elimelech decided to pack up his family and move to the land of Moab. Most scholars believe that Naomi's husband made a reactionary choice (not a faith-filled one) to move his family to Moab. There's no evidence in Scripture that God prompted or inspired this move. In fact, the Moabites were enemies of the Jews. They were known for their blatant idolatry, for open immorality, and for sacrificing their children to the gods.

Think about this for a moment: Naomi and Elimelech lived as *God's people* in Bethlehem. When the famine hit, as God's own dear children, they could've, should've seen themselves as part of the greater kingdom story.

Bethlehem means house of bread![1] And God's people were out of bread.

This was a time for earnest, fervent prayer, for seeing themselves and their personal needs in the greater story God was writing on the earth at that time: *Have we missed You, God? We cry out to You not only for our family but also for our homeland.*

Search our hearts. Show us Your way. Be our great provider and deliverer. We humble ourselves before You and cry out to You! We need You this day and every day!

What did Elimelech do? He kept his problems and his needs in the smaller story and grabbed a self-serving solution that met a short-term need but at a long-term cost. In the end, Elimelech's choice turned their lives upside down. In other words, he led his family outside of God's intended will and protective boundaries, and they suffered grave consequences as a result.

Can you relate? Have you ever—in reaction to your fears or to a desperate need—grabbed first and prayed later? How did that turn out for you?

We live in a fast-paced world chock-full of microwave, click-of-a-button answers. If we have a need or experience an uncomfortable circumstance, we can grab for ourselves a temporary solution before the day is over.

Yet at what cost to ourselves and to our story? And at what cost to those God intended us to influence? We so often forget that God uses us not only through the blessings He's entrusted to us, but also through the needs He allows in our lives, needs that are intended to compel us to pray bigger prayers than we'd typically pray.

In our times of blessing and need, God intends to bless the world through us.

In our times of blessing and in our times of need, God intends to bless the world through us. We're always a part of a bigger story than our own immediate needs, hardships, and problems initially reveal. If we can remember as much, we'll view our lives through God's eternal lens and develop an expectancy that He'll not only come through *for us*, He'll use our hardship to bless the world *through us*.

Dr. Warren Wiersbe, one of my favorite Bible scholars, offers this great insight:

> When trouble comes to our lives, we can do one of three things: endure it, escape it, or enlist it. If we only *endure* our trials, then trials become our master, and we have a tendency to become hard and bitter. If we try to *escape* our trials, then we will probably miss the purposes God wants to achieve in our lives. But if we learn to *enlist* our trials, they will become our servants instead of our masters and work for us; and God will work all things together for our good and for His glory (Romans 8:28).[2]

Naomi's husband eventually dies. Her sons get married. And they settle in the land of Moab with people who live, believe, and perceive life from an ungodly, worldly perspective. After about a decade, Naomi's sons also die, leaving her with two grieving Moabite daughters-in-law. Imagine what that must have been like for Naomi. She's in a foreign land, alone, widowed, feeling forsaken, totally disillusioned, and completely heartbroken. One theologian said that Naomi's husband traded one famine for three funerals.

Naomi wasn't just a grieving widow and mother; she lived in a foreign land and found herself suddenly vulnerable to poverty, abuse, and injustice. You can only imagine why she's so distraught and how deeply her fear and heartbreak must impact her.

She hears through the grapevine that the famine has ended in Bethlehem and she determines to make the trek back home. Some scholars believe that Naomi decided to return to Bethlehem once again to meet an immediate need for food, not necessarily because she wanted to be back in the center of God's will for her. Whether she's grabbing a quick solution for herself or has come to her senses amidst her grief, she decides to return to her homeland.

I tend to think Naomi is too distraught to consider the bigger picture at this point. She learns that Bethlehem has bread.

She needs old friends and family around her. So she decides to make the long journey home. Naomi still acknowledges God's involvement in the lives of people, but it seems she thinks He's forgotten about *her*. Oh, my heart breaks for her! When we unexpectedly lose what we love, we run the risk of also losing sight of the God who loves us.

I cannot fathom the kind of grief Naomi must have felt in her soul. At this point it seems that while Naomi still acknowledges God, she sees Him more as distant and involved by chance. The reason I don't believe that she's yet arrived at that place of open-handed surrender is because of what she says to her daughters-in-law prior to her departure. Let's read this exchange:

> So she departed from the place where she was, and her two daughters-in-law with her; and they went on the way to return to the land of Judah. And Naomi said to her two daughters-in-law, "Go, return each of you to her mother's house. May the LORD deal kindly with you as you have dealt with the dead and with me. May the LORD grant that you may find rest, each in the house of her husband." Then she kissed them, and they lifted up their voices and wept.
>
> Ruth 1:7–9 NASB

At first glance, Naomi's desire for her girls seems noble. She clearly loves them and doesn't want to be a burden to them. She wants them to have another chance at marriage and motherhood.

But if you scoot in a little closer, you'll see something critical here, something that I don't want us to miss. Naomi's God is the God of Abraham, Isaac, and Jacob—the one true God, the creator of the heavens and the earth, of all that is seen and unseen. In essence, she's encouraging her dear daughters-in-law this way:

Go back to your families, to the land of idolatry. The tangible security you'll find there is far greater than anything my

God can or will supply for you. In fact, the hand of the Lord is so clearly against me, He has nothing to offer you. Go back to your homeland, your families, and your idols, for that's the best you can hope for.

Initially, both women protest and insist on going with Naomi, but eventually Naomi's daughter-in-law Orpah heeds her mother-in-law's advice and stays in Moab. We never hear from her again.

But apparently, over the course of ten years, Naomi's faith had deeply impacted her other daughter-in-law, because Ruth's response bursts with faith, conviction, and courage. Read her powerful words to Naomi:

> But Ruth replied, "Don't ask me to leave you and turn back. Wherever you go, I will go; wherever you live, I will live. Your people will be my people, and your God will be my God. Wherever you die, I will die, and there I will be buried. May the LORD punish me severely if I allow anything but death to separate us!" When Naomi saw that Ruth was determined to go with her, she said nothing more.
>
> Ruth 1:16–18 NLT

Ruth's courage and conviction challenge me from the top of my head to the tips of my toes. Think about the implications of Ruth's declaration. She is willing to risk a dangerous trip to a foreign land, to live among people who will surely judge her as an ungodly outsider. Imagine how the Jewish women will treat the new Moabite in town. They'll whisper as she walks by. They'll judge her for the sins of her people. They'll consider her used up and discarded for intermarrying with one of their own.

Yet Ruth was willing to leave all that she knew for a God she could not see. She risked physical safety, emotional security, and relational familiarity for her spiritual destiny. Isn't that just amazing? Somehow, some way, over the years, Naomi's sincere

41

faith sowed seeds into the soil of Ruth's soul, enough so that when Naomi's heart was utterly broken, she could borrow the faith of a young woman who now loved God for herself.

Destructive Disappointment

Naomi battled destructive disappointment. Ever been there? I sure have. Here's how I define destructive disappointment: *Rehashing your losses and unfulfilled expectations in a way that damages you and causes you harm (and negatively impacts your relationships).*

When we're smack in the midst of our disappointments, we stare at the barren field that we expected to produce a bounty of fruit, and we wonder:

Why didn't this field produce fruit?

I planted seeds. I watered them with the Word. I lived by faith. Why am I not seeing the results You promised me?

What. Happened. Lord?

Maybe you can relate:

- Maybe your marriage isn't what you thought it would be
- Or your marriage ended and you didn't want it to
- Your kids aren't going the way you trained them to go
- You battle chronic illness though you took great care of yourself
- Your closest friendship failed and you don't know why
- Your finances are a mess though you've faithfully paid your bills, tithed, and tried to live by faith
- Maybe you faithfully served at church and you've been replaced with little or no explanation
- Maybe you lost a job that you absolutely loved
- Or you lost a parent, a child, your spouse, or your house

It's tempting to ask the *why* and the *how* questions. But if we stay stuck in the whys and the hows, we forget to look up. At some point along the way, we need to step back from asking the whys and the hows and ask the far more important questions, for these are the questions that will bring life back to our perspective and power back into our prayers:

- What is this disappointment saying to me that's not true?
- What is this disappointment saying about me that's not true?
- What is this disappointment saying to me about God that's not true?

Whenever there's an opportunity for destructive disappointment, there's also an opportunity for divine appointments.

Naomi believed that God's hand was against her, when in truth, she and her family had walked outside of God's will for their lives and suffered grave consequences. Then she blamed God (which I've done too).

She believed the lie that God had set out to destroy her, when in truth, amidst her wandering ways, He'd already made a plan to redeem her story.

Naomi believed that God had sent her out empty-handed, when in truth, her story was far from over and she had completely misjudged God and misinterpreted her pain.

We must remember that whenever God allows our hands to be empty for a season, it's because He intends to fill them.

Speak Life

You and I both know what it is to speak out of our pain, wouldn't you say? When our hearts have been hijacked and broken, the enemy smuggles in a lie, and as a result, we say things about ourselves, about our life, and about our God that we don't necessarily mean.

On one hand, there's grace for the broken and the hurting. But that doesn't mean that anything goes when we're disappointed or hurt. In fact, that mind-set will get us into far more trouble than we can imagine. When we consider the utter power in our words, we're wise *not* to give our minds or mouths free rein when our hearts are broken in two.

Not to say we shouldn't process our emotional turmoil with godly, wise friends. But that's quite different than thinking that because we're hurting, we can say anything we want, whenever we want, without consequence.

Lord, help me to be wise with my words when my heart is broken. Help me to speak life, not death. I refuse to speak words in agreement with the very enemy of my soul. He aims to kill. You intend to save and restore and redeem. I stand on Your truth. Help me to speak life about my life, my circumstances, and my future. You have me, Lord, and You'll not let me go.

God is always good. His promises are always true. And even when certain chapters of our lives seem to fly in the face of His promises so much so that we spout off about His seeming forgetfulness or neglect, He still stays very much involved, very much in love, and very much attentive to our redemptive story. Blessed be His name!

I decided to tackle disappointment early on in this book on prayer because this is the place where we so quickly lose our way, our perspective, and our handle on who we are to God and who He is to us.

Going into the storms of life, if we can know that we are His children, His heirs, His prized possessions, we'll stand more sturdily on His truths when the storms hit. And, we'll learn to live and pray with expectancy amidst those storms, because we'll know in the depths of our souls that God wastes nothing and allows nothing that He can't use, redeem, restore, and repurpose for His name's sake.

Grab a cup of coffee or tea and soak in these beautiful words from Jen Pollock Michel:

God is very much involved, very much in love, and very much attentive to our redemptive story.

> Prayer is the courageous act of bringing our authentic desires before God. Prayer is the place where, in Jesus' name, we meet a holy God with all of our humanity hanging out. In our bravest moments of unscripted, unedited prayer, we find ourselves telling God what we want, how we're afraid to want this, how we fear he'll withhold, how we fail to trust and to worship and to reverence. We allow ourselves to see—and be seen. In this struggle, prayerful and raw, we willingly wait for the mercies of God to deliver us into the abiding belief that he is good. Prayer, bold and beautiful and brave, takes on the quality of our struggle to surrender to the God who is holy, to the God whose holiness produces our surprise.[3]

A Blessing for You

May God, right here, right now, grant you abundant grace and a right perspective. May He instill in your heart and mind new courage to stand strong and think long. May you, amidst your hardships, remember who you are. May you, as you move forward from this place, pray powerful prayers based on God's goodness and your connection to Him. You are His. He is yours. Dare to stand in faith and hang on until the storm passes. Soon the sun will break through the clouds and Jesus will bring clarity to your soul. Until then, trust God and remember that He is good even when life is hard.

Let's Pray . . .

*Precious Lord, thank You for Your heart for me! Though
I tend to take my cues from my circumstances, You have
called me to a higher way. Open my eyes once again to
Your significant involvement in my life. Awaken my heart
once again to the power of Your name. Help me to see that
these battles I face are achieving in me a glory that reflects
Your image. May I lean in and learn, draw deep and trust,
and pray hard and believe, because You are here with me,
You are true to Your Word, and in due time I will see a
breakthrough. You are good no matter what my circumstances try to say to me. Hard times will come and hard
times will go, but Your love is mine and Your name is true.
Thank You, King Jesus. My heart trusts in You! Amen.*

Praying God's Word

Write out a personalized prayer and weave in the truths of
the following Scripture. Make the declaration that no matter
what you're facing right now, God is writing a bigger story with
your life, and your circumstances will not have the last say!

Therefore we do not lose heart. Though outwardly we are wasting away, yet inwardly we are being renewed day by day. For our
light and momentary troubles are achieving for us an eternal
glory that far outweighs them all. So we fix our eyes not on what
is seen, but on what is unseen, since what is seen is temporary,
but what is unseen is eternal.

2 Corinthians 4:16–18

A POWERFUL WORD: *Anything's Possible*

Do you want to blow the roof off your prayers? Do you want to see impact, life transformation, and blessing that you never thought possible? Do you want to receive God-sized, kingdom-level answers to your prayers? Then pull your prayers from the pages of God's incredible, inspired, and anointed prayer book. Commit right now to make your Bible the center of your prayer life.[4]

Personal Reflection

1. When you consider life's disappointments and heartbreaks, which ones are still fresh for you?

2. Have you ever found yourself in the cycle of destructive disappointment? How long did it take for you to break free from the cycle of your destructive thoughts? Was there a passage of Scripture that anchored you to God's heart for you?

3. The next few questions will take some thoughtful reflection: What have your disappointments said *to you* that are not true?

4. What have your disappointments said *about you* that are not true?

5. What have your disappointments said *to you about God* that are not true?

6. Since you are in Christ, who are you? What are you? (Hint: See 2 Corinthians 5:17; Romans 8:17.)

7. How might God want you to reframe your perspective so you can pray humbly and boldly in faith?

Group Reflection

1. Talk about a time in your life when a circumstance almost derailed your faith and your perspective of God.

2. What did it take for you to find your footing again?

3. What did you learn from that battle?

4. How do you stand differently in a life-storm now?

5. What advice do you have for the person who is right now in the midst of a significant trial, and they're wondering about the reality of God's love?

6. What current circumstances tempt you to doubt God's goodness? Explain.

7. Which passages of Scripture serve as your go-to verses that help you stand in the storms?

3

Dare to Pray With Endurance

When Your Heart Breaks

With the goodness of God to desire our highest welfare, the wisdom of God to plan it, and the power of God to achieve it, what do we lack? Surely we are the most favored of all creatures.

A.W. Tozer, *The Knowledge of the Holy*

From the ends of the earth I call to you, I call as my heart grows faint; lead me to the rock that is higher than I.

Psalm 61:2

One particular Mother's Day proved an especially tough one for me. It was a hard day for Kevin too, who stayed in the church foyer to talk with a young man he mentors while I found a seat in the sanctuary. I looked up at the worship team. A couple of the musicians were my son's old friends. These guys were still very much engaged in their faith walk and stayed involved in church life after college. My son moved out of state with a broken heart. Deeply hurt by friendship betrayal, disillusioned with church, and unsure of much of what we call mainstream Christianity, he needed to find answers on his own. He still profoundly loved his family and stayed constantly connected to us, but even so, my heart was utterly broken for him.

Would I ever see him back in this church again? Would we ever stand side by side and raise our hands in worship like we used to? Hard to imagine. At least from my perspective.

Church was packed that morning. Families squished together in the pews. They smiled and whispered back and forth. *Were they making plans for their Mother's Day brunch?* Every which way I turned I saw moms wearing Mother's Day corsages. Surrounded by their kids, old and young, they seemed to genuinely enjoy each other on this festive day. And they worshipped together. My hands rested on each side of me. The available space in the pew squished my heart.

All I've ever wanted out of life was a passionate Christ-following family that does life together. Yet at that very moment, it wasn't mine to have.

My three sons lived in three different states. Though we all loved each other deeply, we were miles apart on that particular day. And the fact that two of them genuinely struggled with their faith meant we were apart in more ways than one.

I looked around and wondered if anybody noticed how lonely I felt. I smoothed out the edges of my dress and rested my hands on the polka-dot hem. Buying this dress was a mistake. I didn't need it. Didn't feel pretty in it.

Oh, to find a small room so I could stop holding my breath and release the sobs that gripped my throat.

Kevin and I raised our sons to passionately love and follow Jesus. And they did—for most of the time they lived under our roof. We laughed a lot during their growing-up years, and we prayed together as a regular way of life. We didn't take ourselves too seriously but we took God very seriously. We had an amazing, wonderful family. Our sons would say the same thing. But once they moved out, two of them wandered in the ways of the world for a time. For the life of me, I couldn't figure out how that happened or what I had done wrong. We weren't legalistic and we weren't inconsistent. We weren't perfect, but we weren't hypocrites either.

But eventually Kevin and I had to let go. We had to give our sons the wings to fly—whether they would soar for Jesus or crash and burn. I now know that each of us has to work out our faith journey and make it our own.

Sitting in that pew, I didn't yet have the holy confidence to fully entrust my sons to God. I didn't know how to find joy in the meantime. My internal heartbreak stood in stark contrast to the smiles on the faces that surrounded me.

In truth, my three sons are good men, hard workers, and amazing husbands. They love their wives, love each other, love their parents, and they love God. They were just finding their way out on their own, and looking back, I'm grateful they felt secure enough to do life honestly in front of us.

My Perspective, My Problem

My problem was my perspective. And it about swallowed me whole on that Mother's Day.

Isn't it something how, smack dab in the midst of our not-yet seasons, we see people who have the very things we long for?

Maybe you're infertile and everywhere you look you see pregnant women holding their belly and groaning, "I'm pregnant! *Again.*"

Or maybe you long to buy a home of your own, and with every step you take, you bump into folks who complain about their long list of household projects and the cost of their new patio furniture.

Or maybe you struggle with chronic illness, and everywhere you go you see people full of health, zest, and energy complaining about the lame workout they just had.

Or maybe you're single and you long to be married. And your co-worker constantly complains about having to pick up after her husband. You listen as she laments, "If I have to pick up one more pair of boxers from the floor, I'm going to lose it." And you think to yourself, *I'd give anything to have to pick up a pair of boxers—if they came with a husband.*

We need to crawl out of our smaller story so we can see all that God is up to in us and around us.

It's like that whack-a-mole game. You don't want to notice, or bump into, or be surrounded by people who have what you want, but they're there. Every. Which. Way. You. Turn. What's a person to do?

Oftentimes our heartaches and our unfulfilled heart's desires skew our perspective and keep us thinking small. We need to learn to crawl out of our smaller story so we can see all that God is up to in and around us. Because He is, and it's awesome.

We Cry Out to God

Last chapter we looked at Naomi's story to help us better understand what to do with our disappointments. Now we'll look at another woman whose heartbreak sent her running into the arms of God. I believe her story will help us more quickly grab hold of our perspective when God's not giving us what we want at the moment. Just wait until you see how God responds to her passionate prayers.

In 1 Samuel we read about Hannah. Dear, sweet Hannah. I love this woman. Her story takes place during the period of the judges. The Israelites found themselves in dire straits because they lacked godly leadership. Political corruption and immorality were rampant. The people were desperate for God's intervention whether they knew it or not.[1] Sound familiar?

Read what Dr. Warren Wiersbe writes about this time and setting:

> As He often did in Israel's history, God began to solve the problem by sending a baby. Babies are God's announcement that He knows the need, cares about His people, and is at work on their behalf. The arrival of a baby ushers in new life and a new beginning; babies are signposts to the future, and their conception and birth is a miracle that only God can do (Gen. 30:1–2). To make the event seem even greater, God sometimes selects barren women to be the mothers, as when He sent Isaac to Sarah, Jacob and Esau to Rebekah, and Joseph to Rachel.[2]

Let's take a peek into Hannah's life and see what we can learn from her. Hannah's husband, Elkanah, loved her. He did. But she was barren. So he married a second wife to give him children. Not really sure why Elkanah didn't look up and seek God for a child through the wife he loved, but for some reason, Elkanah kept himself in the smaller story and grabbed a temporary solution.

Remember what happened when Naomi's husband grabbed for immediate relief instead of redemptive results? Read the last chapter again if you need a refresher. Our short-term solutions will always fall woefully short of God's redemptive plan. And those short-term solutions will often cause us more trouble than we ever bargained for.

Elkanah's extra wife, or second wife, was named Peninnah. I'll call her Penny for short. I'm not a fan of Penny. In fact, she irritates me to no end. I've had to forgive her a few times while studying this passage.

Hannah was barren. Penny was fertile. Hannah loved God and longed for children. But at the moment, her arms remained empty, and her heart broken.

Penny had no trouble getting pregnant. She gave Elkanah a family and then spitefully lorded that family over Hannah. The Bible says she made Hannah's life miserable.

Can you even imagine what that must have been like for Hannah? She loved her husband. Desired to give him a family. Yet she watched his extra wife provide for her husband the very things she longed for. And to make matters worse, Penny repeatedly flaunted her blessing in front of Hannah.

Can you picture it? Hannah's lips quivering with sadness. Penny's lips puckering as she sticks out her tongue with pride. Ugh.

Hannah was a godly woman with a heartbreak. Penny was a spoiled woman with an attitude. Barrenness equaled shame in biblical times. And to have your husband's "other" wife rub it in your face seemed intolerable.

Each year Elkanah traveled with his family to Shiloh to worship at the tabernacle. Let's read *The Message* paraphrase of this story from 1 Samuel:

> Every year this man went from his hometown up to Shiloh to worship and offer a sacrifice to God-of-the-Angel-Armies. . . . When Elkanah sacrificed, he passed helpings from the sacrificial meal around to his wife Peninnah and all her children, but he always gave an especially generous helping to Hannah because he loved her so much, and because God had not given her children. But her rival wife taunted her cruelly, rubbing it in and never letting her forget that God had not given her children. This went on year after year. Every time she went to the sanctuary of God she could expect to be taunted. (vv. 3–7)

Elkanah blessed Hannah with an extra portion because he loved her. Penny cursed Hannah, most likely out of jealousy because Elkanah loved her so much. Scoot in a little closer and consider Hannah's situation: *Hannah was blessed because she was loved. But she felt cursed because she was barren.*

Have you ever felt that way? Have you ever gone through a season where, in your head, you knew you were loved by God, but in your heart, you felt absolutely cursed by Him? Hang with me. Though each of us will walk through the valley of the shadow, God is always with us. And it matters deeply how we steward our perspective, especially when God isn't giving us what our heart so longs for. Back to the story:

> Hannah was reduced to tears and had no appetite. Her husband Elkanah said, "Oh, Hannah, why are you crying? Why aren't you eating? And why are you so upset? Am I not of more worth to you than ten sons?" So Hannah ate. Then she pulled herself together, slipped away quietly, and entered the sanctuary. (vv. 8–10)

What does Hannah do with her heartbreak? She pulls herself together, slips away quietly, and enters the sanctuary.

There, Hannah cries out to God in her anguish. God invites us to do the same.

Bless Hannah's heart. Right in the midst of her guttural sobs and heartfelt cries, the priest Eli asks her if she's been drinking. Drinking! Can you believe it? Picture her weeping before the Lord, and imagine Eli so totally disengaged from the moment that he wonders if the woman is drunk.

This poor girl can't catch a break. Even so, she humbly responds to the priest and explains that she is not intoxicated but, instead, is sincerely praying to the Most High God. Thankfully, Eli believed her. Here's what he says: "Go in peace, and may the God of Israel grant you what you have asked of him" (1 Samuel 1:17).

In due time, Hannah becomes pregnant. She actually feels life flutter in her womb. Imagine. Still, at this point, what she doesn't yet realize is that her very own heartbreak mirrored a greater desire in God's heart.

Her heartbreak, my heartbreak, and your heartbreak, they're meant to inspire passionate prayer *in us and through us* because God is working ALL things together for His purposes.

God invites us to lift our chins, to look to Him, and seek the greater purpose in our suffering. You know why? Because we can be absolutely assured that God has a greater, grander purpose in motion than we can ever fathom or even imagine.

For Hannah, she gave birth to Samuel, who became one of the greatest prophets of the Bible. Read Jack Hayford's powerful insight on Hannah's life:

> God uses the burden of Hannah's heart to bring a surprisingly larger solution to a burden of His own heart. *Barrenness was not only Hannah's condition, but Israel's condition as well.* It was a season of spiritual need and with little prophetic activity, and God sought a voice to speak on His behalf to His people. Hannah could not know that her intense intercession for a child was moving in concert with God—bringing her a son, but also bringing forth the will and blessing of God for a whole nation. *As she entrusts the longings of her heart to God, He moves on her behalf, but also advances His larger plan through her at the same time.*[3]

In the midst of our not-yet seasons and times of heartbreak and disappointment, we must remember there are aspects of our story that are significant to the greater story God is writing on the earth today—things that though we can't see with our eyes right now are nevertheless in motion in the heavenly realm to bring about the purposes of Almighty God.

One day when our faith becomes sight and we see clearly all He's been up to, we'll so wish we had trusted Him fully. When we see how the temporary death of our dream brought life to a multitude of others, we'll long for another chance to fully engage our faith. So let's engage our faith *now*. Today.

When we look up from our heartbreak and discern how it mirrors on a bigger scale what's going on in the world today, we suddenly become a prayerful force to reckon with.

Dare to ask yourself this question: *As I pray passionately and pour out my heart to God, could it be that my prayers are moving in concert with God to bring about His greater purposes on the earth today?*

God is nearer than we discern and He's always writing a bigger story than we can see at the moment. Yet it's hard to believe when our hearts are breaking. It's hard to believe when the field, or our womb, or our bed, or the pew, is empty at the moment.

The enemy hopes beyond hope that we'll keep ourselves in the smaller story, keep thinking of ourselves as empty-handed orphans, because if, for even a moment, we remember who and Whose we are and what we have access to . . . well, we'll become downright dangerous in prayer.

> The one concern of the devil is to keep the saints from praying. He fears nothing from prayerless studies, prayerless work, prayerless religion. He laughs at our toil, he mocks at our wisdom, but he trembles when we pray.[4]

One last thought before we wrap up this chapter. Let's go back again to what Elkanah said to Hannah amidst her heartbreak: "Oh, Hannah, why are you crying? Why aren't you eating? And why are you so upset? Am I not of more worth to you than ten sons?"

One day as I cried out to God for the sake of my own family, the Lord whispered the words in this verse back to me. His question revealed my own idolatry. He asked, *"Am I not better than ten sons?"*

Any gift from God's hand—even those things He deeply desires to give us—pales in comparison to the treasure of knowing His heart. *He* is the greatest gift. Getting what we want from God isn't necessarily the same as experiencing kingdom power amidst our circumstances. It's simply enjoying relief from them. When we:

- Take the right job
- Pay off the bill
- Welcome home a prodigal
- Find a spouse
- Buy a house
- See our marriage restored

All of these things are good gifts from a Father who loves us, but they don't take the place, don't even come close to the treasure, of Jesus Himself. When He grants our requests, we feel relief. That is, until we experience our next need, feel angst over the next heartbreak, and long to see our next breakthrough.

But, if amidst our desperate cries to God for the pain in our soul, we press on to experience the power of the risen Christ and fellowship with Him *right in the midst of* our not-yet season, we find a fullness in Him that no answer to prayer or breakthrough can bring us. And that's what it means for the joy of the Lord to be our strength.

Any gift from God's hand pales in comparison to the treasure of knowing His heart.

What we so often want is to feel relief from our difficult circumstances, but God desires for us to experience His resurrection power amidst those circumstances. For me personally, when it comes to experiencing the resurrection power of

God Himself amidst my not-yet seasons, I feel as though I've been twiddling around in the kiddie pool while the ocean is just a few steps away from me.

Oh, I long to know and experience—right here, right now—the kingdom power that God has freely made available to me. I don't want to get caught up in the cycle of angst and relief, alternately getting my way and complaining when I don't, simply living from one need to the next. I have all I need in Him, and I want to live in the reality of that power both when my heart is full and bursting and when it's broken and bruised.

The more I get to know Christ, the wider the gap becomes between anything this earth has to offer and everything that God has promised. I want to know Him more. I feel quite sure that you do too.

> I want to know Christ and experience the mighty power that raised him from the dead. I want to suffer with him, sharing in his death, so that one way or another I will experience the resurrection from the dead!
>
> Philippians 3:10–11 NLT

A Blessing for You

> May God give you a fresh revelation of His great love for you. May the veil between heaven and earth seem especially thin during this season of your life. Jesus came to earth to save you so that you, as a redeemed soul, can live forever with Him. Though you have troubles, you will triumph because Jesus says so. Keep walking. Keep praying. Keep asking. Keep believing. You're not alone. You're not under your circumstances. You're under His wing and He's got you.

Let's Pray . . .

Precious Father, there is something of You that I've yet to experience, especially in the areas of my greatest desires, my deepest needs, and my most profound heartbreaks. Everything I long for is found in You. The things I stare at, the things I fixate on (as legitimate as they are) are far inferior to You. Simply You, Lord. The angst I feel reveals a misplaced desire of my heart. The answer for my angst isn't that I finally receive what I ask for. The answer for my angst right here, right now, is found in the Person of Jesus Christ, my Lord, my Savior, my Prince of Peace. I turn from my soul unrest, and I delight, in a much deeper way, in the presence and the power of Almighty God. I seek You first and foremost, knowing I'll find You faithful. Take me to that river of delight so I can know You in ways I've never known possible. You are so faithful, Lord. I entrust my cares and concerns to You, and I press on to better know Your heart. Amen.

Praying God's Word

Write out a personalized prayer and weave in the truths of the following Scripture. Ask God to give you His perspective on your life, your trials, and the greater purpose He's working out in your life.

And we know that God causes everything to work together for the good of those who love God and are called according to his purpose for them.

Romans 8:28 NLT

A POWERFUL WORD: *More of Jesus*

As you give up the life you thought you needed, you'll find yourself getting more of God Himself. And He will so satisfy your heart that all other passions will be consumed by your longing for Him.[5]

Personal Reflection

1. What unfulfilled longing is in your heart right now?

2. What are the most consistent kinds of prayers you've prayed around this situation (e.g., faith-filled, begging-pleading, lament, surrendered, etc.)?

3. What do you sense God is saying to you in this season?

4. How might your heartbreak reflect God's heart for what's going on in our world today (e.g., broken marriages, prodigals, financial upheaval, loneliness, sickness, etc.)?

5. Envision that angst in your heart turning into passion in your soul—a passion not only for your story, but also for the many who struggle the way you do. Can you imagine becoming a mighty prayer warrior for the greater burden on *God's* heart today?

6. Picture yourself right this moment, rolling your cares off of your shoulders and into God's hands. God is bigger than our hurts, our fears, our hopes, and our dreams. Write out a faith-filled prayer declaring that beautiful truth.

7. Part of what it means to renew our perspective is simply to get a right perspective. Are there parts of your story

that you may see disproportionately? Have your friends or loved ones challenged your perspective? Dare to ask God to give you eyes to see with clarity so your heart can pray with accuracy.

Group Reflection

1. Share about a time when amidst a difficult season or circumstance, God intervened and gave you a fresh perspective.

2. How did that encounter change the way you approached your circumstances?

3. What does your default response tend to be when hard times come?

4. What challenging circumstances have you been praying about these days?

5. What is God saying to you in this particular season?

6. Share about a time when God came through for you and was faithful to you in spite of your own perspective.

7. Are you open to experiencing God in a way you never have before? And does that question make you excited or uncomfortable? Explain.

4

Dare to Pray and Say What's True

When You Forget Who You Are

The reason we are more than we know is because God is greater than we can imagine.

Patsy Clairmont, *You Are More Than You Know*

This resurrection life you received from God is not a timid, grave-tending life. It's adventurously expectant, greeting God with a childlike "What's next, Papa?" God's Spirit touches our spirits and confirms who we really are. We know who he is, and we know who we are: Father and children. And we know we are going to get what's coming to us—an unbelievable inheritance!

Romans 8:15–16 The Message

Ever had one of those weeks when everything that could go wrong does go wrong? You can't find your groove to save your life and your circumstances repeatedly trip you up and stress you out? I'd be surprised if you said no. And more than a little impressed.

I remember one such week for me. I battled insomnia in the worst way, which made me feel prickly all over. My children were out of sorts too. They were under the weather and crabby and seemed to cry over the littlest things. I felt irritable and easily frustrated. And so tired that my skin hurt. If I didn't trip over a toy or pair of shoes, I'd drop something. And you know? It's kind of pathetic when you trip over absolutely nothing while holding something in your hand. But I somehow managed to do that as well.

At one point I passed by a mirror and winced. I didn't at all like the reflection staring back at me. Not one bit. I saw only the worst version of myself. Crabby. Exhausted. Brain-fogged. Which was especially uncomfortable since I had a speaking event coming up that weekend.

How could I possibly prepare my heart when I couldn't even find my footing? But then, deep within my soul, I sensed God's invitation to trust Him with the surface parts of me, things that I could barely stand to acknowledge, as well as to trust Him with the deepest parts of me that still needed healing and wholeness.

Amidst the temptation to loathe myself and cringe at my weakness, I put my foot down and prayed: "Lord, even here, even now, I belong to You. And despite my bleary eyes and messy hair, I'm still Your treasure—a spoken-for heir of God. This is true because You say it's true. So I speak it out loud for my own ears to hear, and I choose to believe it until my heart fully knows it. Thank You, thank You for seeing past my frazzled exterior and for valuing the treasure of my soul. I wrap my arms around Your grace. I seek Your face in this place. And I will finish this race because You promised to get me safely home. In Jesus' name, I pray, Amen."

Then I felt an inner whisper, a nudge, to open the Bible to 2 Corinthians 4:13. Now please let me qualify something here: This doesn't always happen. I don't regularly receive a pointed direction to Scripture, but I do every once in a while, so I listen closely when such nudges come to me. Here's the passage I looked up that particular day:

> It is written: "I believed; therefore I have spoken." Since we have that same spirit of faith, we also believe and therefore speak. . . .
>
> 2 Corinthians 4:13

Read the second part of that verse again: *Since we have that same spirit of faith, we also believe and therefore speak.* We *do* believe, and therefore *speak.* The word *speak* translates this way:[1]

- *Declare*
- *Speak out*
- *Speak forth*
- *Proclaim*
- *Tell*
- *Utter*

First, we dare to believe; we grab God's truth as our very own. Then, amidst our choice to believe, we walk and talk like it's true.

When faith makes its way into our ears, it also finds its way into our hearts. In my experience, when my ears hear my mouth say truths that God has reflected in His Word, I'm changed. I'm strengthened. And I remember once again that I'm not who I was. I'm not what I do. I'm someone God loves and enjoys.

As we go through life, we'll walk through storms that smash against us. We'll try to find our footing amidst the pelting rain and the whipping winds. Sometimes those storms are of our own making. Sometimes they're the natural elements of a fallen world. And sometimes we're turned upside down in a storm that had nothing to do with us and everything to do with someone else's rotten choices.

No matter the reason for the storm, at times we'll find our-selves responding in ways that are beneath us. We'll say things we wish we hadn't. We'll be forced to reckon with our humanity and with our very real need for a Savior.

Praise God we have one!

During such times it helps if we remind our souls that we love because He loved us first. We can walk in His promises, not because we're perfect, but because He is. We can enjoy His presence because He's the One who invited us there in the first place. We can and will be used greatly by Him because He knew all about our frailties long before we were ever aware of them, and He planned ahead of time to redeem us from them.

To the degree that we admit our desperate need for more of Jesus, we will encounter and experience more of Jesus. But this dark, devastating secret always comes into play: The enemy loves nothing more than to see us sulk in our humanity. Thankfully, our heavenly Father loves nothing more than to see us soar because of His promise of eternity!

We can walk in His promises, not because we're perfect, but because He is.

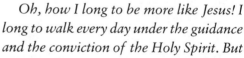

Oh, how I long to be more like Jesus! I long to walk every day under the guidance and the conviction of the Holy Spirit. But thanks be to God that even when I trip up, He doesn't disgustedly look the other way. He loves me today. He's willing to use me mightily today. He dares to write my name on His hand. He's written His name on my heart, and He claims me as one of His own. There is no one like our God! I will believe. I do believe. I will, therefore, speak with boldness and great power.

We Are Weak, He Is Strong

So I went to my speaking engagement weak-kneed but strong in heart. And God moved mightily in our midst—collectively in that place and specifically in our hearts! After my session, women from all different walks of life waited to tell me their own powerful stories.

One particular treasured soul waited in line for an extended time. But when she finally got to me, she couldn't find her words. With clenched fists and stiff arms, she tightened her lips and made herself look at me. I stood there for a moment and prayerfully waited for her to speak. Finally she did. With her feet firmly planted, she guardedly said, "No words. I don't have anything to say."

I carefully asked, "How about if I give you a hug?"

She barely nodded, but that was enough of an invitation for me. I wrapped my arms around her and became instantly aware of something the Lord wanted to say to her.

"A new name," I whispered. Then I backed up, grabbed her shoulders, looked her in the eyes, and said, "The Lord wants to give you a *new* name."

Her jaw dropped. She glanced around to see if anyone had noticed her. She squeezed her eyes shut and tears rolled down her face. She began to tremble and shake. Her lips quivered as she fought for her words. She didn't move from her spot. But she didn't say anything either.

I felt strongly led to continue, so I did. "Whatever past labels have been a reproach to you, God is going to remove from you. He is giving you a new name. He is writing a new song on your heart and He is bringing you into a new land."

Still trembling, she suddenly didn't seem to care so much who noticed her. She wrapped her arms around me and squeezed the breath out of me. Then she backed up slightly, but still close enough to share under her breath, "I didn't want to come to this conference. I don't relate to these women. I'm going through a divorce. My husband is in prison for sexually abusing our children. I'm still wearing his name, and it has been an utter reproach to me. I was kicked out of the church choir because of *his* name and *his* choices. I had a painful childhood and didn't want to go back to my maiden name. What I want more than anything in the whole world . . . is a new name."

Absolutely stunned by God's great grace in both of our lives, I suddenly knew on a deeper level how important it was for me to really grasp and know who I am in Christ, so I can help others know who they are too.

> I waited patiently for the LORD; he turned to me and heard my cry. He lifted me out of the slimy pit, out of the mud and mire; he set my feet on a rock and gave me a firm place to stand. He put a new song in my mouth, a hymn of praise to our God. Many will see and fear the LORD and put their trust in him.
>
> Psalm 40:1–3

I've learned that to the extent that I seek to know *this love*— this unending, otherworldly, unrelenting love of Jesus—in a way that's absolutely personal *to me*, I will walk and talk and pray and give and live in the fullness He intended *for me*. And to the extent that I dare to believe that His love is divinely intimate and profoundly powerful for me, others will more likely grasp it when they encounter me. To know this love is to be filled with the fullness of God.

> For this reason I kneel before the Father, from whom every family in heaven and on earth derives its name. I pray that out of his glorious riches he may strengthen you with power through his Spirit in your inner being, so that Christ may dwell in your hearts through faith. And I pray that you, being rooted and established in love, may have power, together with all the Lord's holy people, to grasp how wide and long and

high and deep is the love of Christ, and to know this love that surpasses knowledge—that you may be filled to the measure of all the fullness of God.

Ephesians 3:14–19

Established in Love

Are you rooted and established in love? I don't always feel like I am. Don't always believe that I am. But because I'm in Christ, I'm established in Him! And because you're in Christ, you are too! The goal is to walk in, talk in, and live in the reality of God's love, a love that grounds us and establishes us regardless of the storms we face.

To be filled to the measure of all the fullness of God, to be filled to the spilling-over brim with the all-surpassing love of Christ, is to be transformed from the inside out; it's to dare to come boldly into God's great presence and to ask Him for the impossible, unachievable, inconceivable, and unbelievable. Because this is what heirs do. We use our high status and privilege to access our inherited riches so we can address the needs before us, and in us, and around us. Prayer links us in fellowship with almighty God. His promises belong to us.

We're not spoiled children who get what we want when we want it. We don't have a spineless father who comes running when we stomp our feet, who gives in to our every whim. Our great God is the King of Kings, Lord of Lords, and General of all generals. He's intimately involved, profoundly patient, and wonderfully true. He is wise, all-knowing, good, and kind. He leads us up mountains, through valleys, and through the storms.

He knows what we need more than we do and will time out His answers and breakthroughs in a way that strengthens our faith, sturdies our stance, and softens our heart.

Nobody cares for our heart, our soul, and our story like God does. He never forgets about us. Never looks the other way. Never ceases to love us. Even when we're unlovable.

But far too often *we* forget who we are. We derive our joy, our perspective, and our sense of value from our behavior and our performance. We sometimes forget that we belong to Jesus. We forget that we lack no good thing. It slips our mind that we are rich in every way *so* we can be generous on every occasion.

In spite of all of our sleepless nights, our crabby days, our broken hearts, and the wounds we endure at the hands of others, we must not forget this important, immovable truth: We are heirs, children of God, deeply loved and profoundly cared for.

When we catch our messy selves praying and pleading from underneath our circumstances, it's time to remind our souls of His love. To know this love is to be filled with the fullness of God.

In Christ, you're not a slightly improved version of yourself. You're something altogether new, lovely, redeemed, and blessed.

God will time out His answers and breakthroughs in a way that strengthens our faith, sturdies our stance, and softens our heart.

Jesus invites you into His inner court to talk with Him, tell Him what you need, and share the concerns of your heart. And you can rest assured that He's always glad to see you.

Don't race through life's moments forgetting who you are. Heir "amnesia" will not only deprive you of the thriving life to which your soul is heir, it'll also keep you from spilling life onto those around you who desperately need to know how the Father feels about them. You have access for a purpose: to walk intimately with a loving-living God, and to reflect His love to a world very much in need.

A Blessing for You

As you walk through your everyday life, dare to scoot a little closer to Jesus, cup your ear, and listen to what He has to say to you. He loves you. He cherishes you. He has hopes for you. He wants to heal you, restore you, and renew you. His truth will set you free. His power will part the waters. His love will heal your soul. His heart for you will make you whole. Lean in today. Listen for His voice—His gentle, powerful, redemptive, and life-giving voice. Oh, how He loves you! May you dare to believe who you can be because of Him. Have a blessed and beautiful day.

Let's Pray . . .

Precious Father, I believe! Forgive my unbelief! I want to walk in Your presence as I live here on earth. Help me to better know and understand Your love. Increase my capacity to grasp Your goodness. Reveal to me the parts of Your character that I don't fully understand. I want to live full and free, abounding in love, full of expectant hope. I want to pray with a heart that knows You're good and that Your promises are true. Seep these truths deep into my soul. Awaken fresh purpose and passion in me. And teach me how to speak life into every person and situation I encounter. You brought life to me. Release fresh revelation through me. I want others to experience the love You've so freely given me. You've established me in love. Help me to walk and talk and live and give like it's true. In Jesus' name, I pray, Amen.

Praying God's Word

Write out a personalized prayer and weave in the truths of the following Scripture. Make the declaration that no matter what you're facing right now, nothing can separate you from the love of God!

I pray that out of his glorious riches he may strengthen you with power through his Spirit in your inner being, so that Christ may dwell in your hearts through faith. And I pray that you, being rooted and established in love, may have power, together with all the Lord's holy people, to grasp how wide and long and high and deep is the love of Christ.

Ephesians 3:16–18

A POWERFUL WORD: *Jesus Breathes Life*

And what makes all this hard stuff worth it? Only, always Him. . . . And praise be to Him that just about the time we feel helpless, drowning, incapable of making such a proclamation of wanting Him, He blows in with a hopeful, resuscitating wind and—mouth on mouth—revives us. This is the glory of traveling with the Life—how He breathes vitality in dead spaces and offers His marvelous, illuminating light in places that are dark. And when we're in those dark places, we want God in big heaps and not small portions, because pain doesn't ever truly get better without Him. The more we have of Him, the more we survive and even thrive; the more beauty we extract from life.[2]

Personal Reflection

1. How do you feel about yourself today? How do you suppose your impression lines up with God's thoughts toward you?

2. When was the last time you paused to *remember* how deeply the Father loves you? How about if you spend some time doing so right now?

3. When was the last time you felt especially acquainted with Christ's affection for you? What were the circumstances surrounding that experience?

4. When was the last time you reflected God's heart to another? What were the circumstances surrounding that experience?

5. What desires of your heart have you tucked away and neglected or refused to pray for? How about if you pull those things out right now and pray for them?

6. What kinds of prayers do you think the Father most loves to answer?

7. Do you think He cares about your deepest desires? Why or why not? (Read Psalm 37:23 for a little direction.)

Group Reflection

1. How often do you think about God's love for you? Explain.

2. When was the last time you really sensed His nearness and His love?

3. What circumstances seem to most often block your view of God or your sense of His love? Do you think your perspective is biblical? Explain.

4. What deep desires have you yet to pray for? *Smooth transitions new seasons*

5. Can you remember a time (during a hardship or a mess-up) when you dared to run toward God and pray boldly, even though you were tempted to run away and hide?

6. In what area of life do you desire to know more of God's passion, power, and provision?

7. What needs to change in your perspective of God and your circumstances to actually have faith for a breakthrough?

God, Your Father

So don't be afraid, little flock. For it gives your Father great happiness to give you the Kingdom.

Luke 12:32 NLT

5

Dare to Pray Like an Heir

You're Royalty

I want to spend the rest of my days speaking truth born of a fully convinced heart. God accepts me and radically loves me. He embraces me and calls me His own. Who He is and what He is up to in my life—these things are worth boasting about.

Brady Boyd, *Sons and Daughters*

For all who are led by the Spirit of God are children of God. So you have not received a spirit that makes you fearful slaves. Instead, you received God's Spirit when he adopted you as his own children. Now we call him, "Abba, Father." For his Spirit joins with our spirit to affirm that we are God's children.

Romans 8:14–16 NLT

Often when I speak about the message of our identity in Christ, I'll have two tables on stage: an orphan table and an heir table. Picture the orphan table as a rickety old table that bobbles unevenly on a level floor. The splintered chair wobbles with uneven legs. A stale piece of bread sits on a cracked dinner plate. The very sight of it makes your mouth dry up and your heart ache.

Now picture the heir table. White linen covers the table. A high-back chair displays plush velvet fabric and ornamental cherrywood trim. A crystal vase boasts a bright bouquet of flowers. Polished silverware flanks the decorative china dinnerware. A satin napkin sits wrapped in a gold embossed napkin ring. An assortment of breads is arranged next to a bowl of fresh fruit. The sparkling wine shimmers in a crystal carafe. The very sight of it makes you wonder what these people do for a living.

Now notice the distinction between these two tables.

When we read Scripture, we find that God cares deeply for the poor, the orphan, the misplaced, and the oppressed. That's why He asks those of us who have more to give to those who have less. Time and time again He mentions the poor and asks us to take care of them. That's a part of our kingdom call. Jesus cares about the literal orphans and He wants us to care about them too.

But He also cares deeply about the spiritual orphan. That's why He didn't consider His equality with God a thing to be grasped, leveraged, or used for His benefit. In fact, He stepped away from His high, privileged position in heaven to meet us right where we live. He came to earth in the womb of a vulnerable teenage girl; He came right to us in the very depths of our need.

> Though he was God, he did not think of equality with God as something to cling to. Instead, he gave up his divine privileges; he took the humble position of a slave and was born as a human being. When he appeared in human form, he humbled himself in obedience to God and died a criminal's death on a cross.
>
> Philippians 2:6–8 NLT

Jesus loves and treasures the spiritual orphan. That's why He made a way to adopt us into the family of God. But once we become heirs, He doesn't want us acting or thinking like orphans any longer. Spiritual orphans beg and plead. *Heirs pray and believe.*

Saved by Grace

Did you know that our star-breathing God intimately loves every single person who has ever walked the earth? He created us in His image with a beautiful and specific purpose in mind. And He loves what He has created in you!

Here's an important point to remember: God loves everyone. But that doesn't mean everyone is saved. Though love made a way for us, it's by grace that we're saved.[1] Read the following passage:

> For it is by grace you have been saved, through faith—and this is not from yourselves, it is the gift of God—not by works, so that no one can boast.
>
> Ephesians 2:8–9

Louie Giglio once said, "Your sin doesn't make you bad. It makes you dead." Here's another passage to ponder until it makes you weep with gratitude:

> You were dead in sins, and your sinful desires were not yet cut away. Then he gave you a share in the very life of Christ, for he forgave all your sins, and blotted out the charges proved against you, the list of his commandments which you had not obeyed. He took this list of sins and destroyed it by nailing it to Christ's cross. In this way God took away Satan's power to accuse you of sin, and God openly displayed to the whole world Christ's triumph at the cross where your sins were all taken away.
>
> Colossians 2:13–15 TLB

We've done ourselves a great disservice by preaching an improve-your-life-now kind of gospel message. Truly though, who *doesn't* want to upgrade their life? This kind of message appeals to the consumer in us. However, when our main concern is for a slight-to-moderate improvement in our life here on earth, we miss the essence and the power of the cross of Jesus Christ. We miss the point of our very desperate need for a Savior.

Spiritual orphans beg and plead. Heirs pray and believe.

Consider again the Colossians 2 passage: While we were dead in our sins, Christ died for us. We weren't in need of a slight up-grade, a makeover, or a temporary loan to get us on our feet again. *We were destined for hell.* Dying in our sins. Totally incapable of saving ourselves. And in that place of our utter and desperate need—while our selfishness, sinfulness, and pride remained in full swing—Christ died for us.

I've been pondering this passage a lot lately:

> But, oh, how few believe it! Who will listen? To whom will God reveal his saving power? In God's eyes he was like a tender green shoot, sprouting from a root in dry and sterile ground. But in our eyes there was no attractiveness at all, nothing to make us want him. We despised him and rejected him—a man of sor-rows, acquainted with bitterest grief. We turned our backs on him and looked the other way when he went by. He was despised, and we didn't care.
>
> Isaiah 53:1–3 TLB

It occurred to me the other day that Jesus was

- Despised
- Rejected
- Unattractive
- Overlooked

Why? Because *I'm* despisable, rejectable, and downright unattractive at times. While I have a heart to help the underdog,
I sometimes overlook those in need because I'm thinking only
about myself. Jesus always thought of others, but He wore my
shame just the same.

He was born into poverty and acquainted with every aspect of
who we are because at the very depths of our souls, we are the
poor, sinful, and needy people He came to save. He identified
with our need so He could redeem us completely and profoundly.

People wrongly assessed Jesus (as they still do today), but
He was willing to be misjudged, content to be misunderstood,
because He had us on His mind. Read the rest of this passage
from Isaiah:

> Yet it was *our* grief he bore, *our* sorrows that weighed him down.
> And we thought his troubles were a punishment from God, for
> his *own* sins! But he was wounded and bruised for *our* sins.
> He was beaten that *we* might have peace; he was lashed—and
> we were healed! *We*—every one of us—have strayed away like
> sheep! *We*, who left God's paths to follow our own. Yet God
> laid on *him* the guilt and sins of every one of us!
>
> Isaiah 53:4–6 TLB

Think about it. What Jesus accomplished on the cross was
not simply an invitation to think differently, nor was it a ticket
to a hip Christian social club. Here's the life-changing truth
about Christ's overwhelming victory on the cross:

Jesus' triumph over the grave, over sin and death,
blew the doors off of the enemy's claim on us!

And when we trusted Christ to make us alive in Him, the transformative power of the Holy Spirit took up residence in our soul
and made us brand- new, through and through. The power of the
living God altered our spiritual DNA, changed the trajectory of

our lives, and activated our spiritual genes so that the impossible could now be possible in and through us. Incredible!

This means we're not a slightly improved version of ourselves. Our name is written in the Book of Life! We are citizens of heaven. Heirs of God. Joint heirs with Christ.

I know I'm referencing lots of Scripture in this chapter, but hang with me. Think for a moment about how you feel about yourself, how you talk about yourself when you've blown it. On what basis do you judge yourself? Isn't it most often by your performance? Don't you see that if you view the gospel as a means to an end (good ideas for a better life), you miss the resurrection power that defies gravity, sin, and death? And thus, you misunderstand what is now available to you in Christ Jesus? Read this passage and let it sink deep into your bones:

> Now a slave has no permanent place in the family, but a son belongs to it forever. So if the Son sets you free, you will be free indeed.
>
> John 8:35–36

Do you understand what God has offered us here? We've moved from being orphans to heirs. We have a place at the table of grace! Here's another truth that I want to sink deep into your bones:

In Christ Jesus, there now exists a great chasm between the orphan table and the heir table!

Consider the imagery of the two tables again and answer this question for me: If, once we've become heirs of God, we're part of His family forever, why do we continue to vacillate between these two mind-sets? We sit at the orphan table and beg and plead. And when we've performed well, we more easily picture ourselves at the heir table as if we've somehow earned such a privileged status.

But you are a chosen people, a royal priesthood, a holy nation, God's special possession, that you may declare the praises of him who called you out of darkness into his wonderful light. Once you were not a people, but now you are the people of God; once you had not received mercy, but now you have received mercy.

1 Peter 2:9–10

You're an Heir

In times of despair, we forget that we are heirs. In times of favor, we forget *why* we are heirs.

When life gets hard, or we're not performing like the Christian we feel we should be, we see ourselves at the beggar's table, hoping for a few scraps, thinking we deserve only that much. We tend to shy away from bold prayer, and we either replace it with a good dose of negative self-talk, or we find ourselves whispering those begging types of prayers that leave us feeling small, not loved or embraced like we actually are.

And instead of holding on to these two things . . .

- Identity—*firmly established in the finished work of Christ*
- Humility—*harnessed strength fueled by the Spirit, empowered by His love*

. . . we pick up the virus of spiritual passivity and let it suck the life right out of us.

When we fall short of what we know God deserves from us, we tend to lose our fight for faith because we don't think we have a right to stand in battle. Read this again:

In times of despair, we forget *that* we're heirs.

May you remember today that Jesus' overwhelming victory on the cross gave you a place at the table of grace. You get to be there because Jesus unequivocally defeated sin, death, inferiority, insecurity, imperfection, isolation, and rejection, just to name a few. And He doesn't yank you from your seat at the table when you occasionally lose a battle or forget who you are.

In Christ Jesus, you've been made brand-new, through and through; you're an heir of God, a joint heir with Christ, a royal priest, clothed in righteousness, and dearly beloved. You're anointed and invited to enter the Most Holy of Holies to meet with the star-breathing God who put the galaxies in place. And though He spends His days and hours overseeing the affairs of men, He's never too busy for you. When you approach the throne of grace, you can be assured of God's glad welcome and loving embrace. Why? Because you're one of His own. Always. Forever. No matter what. Isn't that just spectacular? Leaves me speechless.

Read this statement one more time: In times of despair, we forget *that* we're heirs. In times of favor, we forget *why* we're heirs. When we walk through times of favor, we must remember that when life is good, it's because God is good. Every good gift comes from His hand. The enemy would love nothing more than to have us shift our weight onto our works, so he can yank the rug out from under us. Our safest place is at the table of grace—a place we've not earned but that Christ has earned for us. Our only response can be one of humble, awe-inspired gratitude. We rest in the finished work of Christ, and we work from that place of divine privilege. We have nothing to prove and all of eternity to live for.

The more time you spend with Jesus, and the more time you spend pondering His great and personal love for you, the more you'll find that His love heals your soul, makes you whole, and makes your heir status actually believable. What a gift He's given us! And when you pray from that place, everything changes.

A Blessing for You

May God do such a deep healing work in your soul that you're able to look at your disappointments and heartbreaks with a grounded sense of hope and perspective. May your emotions rest on God's immovable, abounding love and faithfulness. May you never again be tossed to and fro by the choices of others and the changes in your circumstances. Your Rock is Christ and He is immovable. Stand on Him. Stand strong because of Him. And know this: one day He'll make your righteousness shine like the dawn and will reveal to the world that you belong to Him! Find your sturdy place of rest in Him today.

Let's Pray . . .

Dear Jesus, I'm only at the beginning stages of understanding what You've actually done for me, actually won for me. Thank You, Lord. Thank You for loving me while I was yet a sinner. Thank You for saving me before I even had a clue what You were actually saving me from. Thank You for giving me a brand-new name, a new identity, and a new power and purpose in life. Thank You for filling me with the power of the Holy Spirit and for sealing my redemption for eternity. I'm an heir. I'm an heir of God because of Your kindness to me! How often I've lived like an orphan because of my own unbelief. Fill me afresh with a sense of Your great love. Awaken my soul to the reality of Your promises. Teach me to walk and talk and pray and give and live like the heir of God I am. I am Yours. I've got everything I need in You, and then some. I'm rich beyond measure, loved beyond comprehension, and equipped to do wonders on the earth by the power of Your Spirit. Do a new thing in me today, Lord. Oh, how I love You!

Praying God's Word

Write out a personalized prayer and weave in the truths of the following Scripture. Make the declaration that no matter what you're facing right now, you are still an heir because you are in Christ Jesus!

> For all who are led by the Spirit of God are children of God. So you have not received a spirit that makes you fearful slaves. Instead, you received God's Spirit when he adopted you as his own children. Now we call him, "Abba, Father."
>
> Romans 8:14–15 NLT

A POWERFUL WORD: *Jesus Is Stronger*

- Light is more powerful than darkness.
- Truth is stronger than error.
- There's more grace in God's heart than sin in men's hearts.
- There's more power in the Holy Spirit to convict men of sin than there is power of satanic forces to tempt men to sin.
- There's more power in one drop of the shed blood of the Lord Jesus to cleanse men's hearts from the stain of sin than there is in the accumulated filth of men's sin since Adam and Eve.[2]

Personal Reflection

1. What kinds of circumstances or choices (or mistakes, or missteps) make you question your heir status?

2. What most helps you find your footing again? How often do you practice that discipline?

3. We tend to pray boldly when we're performing well, and we tend to shrink back when we feel inferior to the call. Why do you suppose we as God's children so often default to and get our perspective from our performance instead of Christ's victory on the cross? Write down your thoughts.

4. The goal is to pray humbly and boldly regardless of our circumstances or our emotional perspective of ourselves at the moment. Write out a prayer asking God to sturdy your sense of status and identity in Him.

5. Write out a declaration of who you are because you are in Christ. (This is only for you; but I suggest you find a few passages of Scripture, write out your own personalized declaration, and preach it to yourself every single day!)

6. When we more deeply grasp our heir status in Christ Jesus, we'll more often pray from a place of divine privilege rather than for it. Now that you have an even firmer grasp on your heir status, how might your prayer life change in the days to come?

7. Identify someone in your life right now who also needs a reminder of his/her treasured status in Christ. Pray a humble, bold prayer on his/her behalf. Ask God to do a wonder-working miracle in his/her life.

Group Reflection

1. Describe a time in your life when you felt especially confident of who you were in Christ. What were the surrounding circumstances?

2. Why did believing come easier to you at that time?

3. Looking back and knowing what you know now, would you say that your performance gave you the *feeling* of a more sturdy identity, or did you actually have a good grasp on who you are in Christ during that time?

4. Why do you suppose we struggle so with our sense of identity in Christ?

5. What do you do to remind your soul of your heir status? How does it impact your perspective and your prayers?

6. Though God loves us whether we pray mousy prayers or mighty prayers, how do you suppose our posture and perspective in prayer affects the outcome of our prayers?

7. Take some time to pray for one another, that you'd all receive a fresh awakening of your precious identity and inheritance in Christ Jesus.

6

Dare to Pray
Without Condemnation

You're Forgiven

Our Lord is more than able to take care of our past. He pardons instantly and forgives completely. His blood makes us worthy— all we are and all we have is by the forgiving love of God!

A.W. Tozer, *I Talk Back to the Devil*

So now there is no condemnation for those who belong to Christ Jesus. And because you belong to him, the power of the life-giving Spirit has freed you from the power of sin that leads to death.

Romans 8:1–2 NLT

I worked in the fitness industry for a number of years before I moved into full-time ministry. Recently, I reconnected with one of my former fitness buddies. I knew her back when she was going through a difficult season in life. We enjoyed catching up. She found faith in Christ since I last saw her, and it's beautiful to see her awaken to His deep love for her. She caught me up on things with her, then she looked me in the eye and said, "I'll never forget how you helped me when I was going through an especially tough time. You gave me that gift of a hundred dollars for groceries, do you remember that?"

I sat back in my chair and thought for a moment, and then replied, "Nope. I don't remember that at all." Then I slapped my hands on my thighs and said, "But do you want to know what I *do* remember? Every single idiotic thing I've ever said and what I was wearing when I said it." We both had a good laugh over that one.

Aren't we so that way? We forget the good things we do and keep a mental record of the bad things we do. And you know what? The devil wants it that way. He dances a jig every time we beat ourselves up over our latest, greatest blunder.

But Jesus? He responds in the opposite way.

- Your sins I remember no more. (Hebrews 8:12)
- Every cup of water you give in My name, I remember, I reward. (Mark 9:41)
- When you talk faith with your fellow believers, I write it down. (Malachi 3:16)

His kindness leads us to fruit-bearing repentance. His goodness makes us grateful. He forgives our sin, rewards us for every act prompted by our faith, cheers for us when we engage our faith, and protects us when we're vulnerable. He uses us in ways totally disproportionate to who we are. He moves when we pray. He allows us glimpses of glory when we've gone too long without seeing the sun.

He grants mercy that redeems, grace that empowers, and life in the Spirit that propels us forward amidst overwhelming odds. That's what He does for His children. He's divinely good and profoundly invested in us.

Now go back to the picture of the orphan and the heir tables. And think back to the last time you tripped up, fell down, and sat your berated self down at the orphan table. Picture yourself there. You hang your head. You kick yourself under the table. You wonder why you just can't get it together. Then you hear the enemy whisper in your ear, *"You sit there and THINK about what you've done!"*

You over-ate—again!

You gossiped—again!

You missed devotions—again!

You don't serve enough—ever!

You don't give enough—ever!

You are NOT enough—ever!

Listen, the devil wants us to trust in our own efforts. Why? So he can accuse us when our own efforts fail us. Of course he wants us to sit there and think about what we've done. What happens when we repeatedly rehash our failures? We begin to believe that we actually *are* failures. What happens when we continuously accuse our own hearts for our not-enough-ness? We find the orphan table a suitable place for us because it fits how we feel about ourselves.

> *What happens when we continuously accuse our own hearts for our not-enough-ness?*

But can you hear your Father's life-giving words to you at that moment? He whispers in your ear, *"Dear one, I don't want you to sit there and think about what you've done!"* Then, with His strong right arm, He points to the royal, beautiful, heir table, the table of grace, and He says to you, *"I want you to sit there and think about what I'VE done!"*

Oftentimes when I give this message at conferences, I pause here and we sing the amazing song "When I Think About the Lord."

Why is it important to *think about the Lord* and *what He's done* for you on a regular basis? Because even though what we do matters deeply, *what Jesus has already done* matters most of all.

When we fail or fall or fumble the ball, the worst thing we can do is stay in the dirt and berate ourselves for our weakness. Why? Because Jesus says it's especially in our weakness that we can know His strength and power.

> Three times I pleaded with the Lord to take it away from me. But he said to me, "My grace is sufficient for you, for my power is made perfect in weakness." Therefore I will boast all the more gladly about my weaknesses, so that Christ's power may rest on me.
>
> 2 Corinthians 12:8–9

So when we've fallen, we should rise again and instantly envision ourselves at the heir table. We should think about all He's done, all He won for you and me. We should ponder anew what the Almighty can do with a soul that will trust in His grace.

Even though what we do matters deeply, what Jesus has already done matters most of all.

Recently, I've leaned in closer to this truth than I ever have before. The moment I say something that is beneath me, the moment I catch myself feeling or acting impatient, suspicious, or unloving, *I think about the Lord.* I look past my weakness and I look to the cross. I remember that my Jesus who died in my place is pure and loving and patient and kind. All the things I'm not, at times. And He has imparted His righteousness to me.

I begin thanking Him for all He's done for me, in me, and for all He's yet to do through me. I praise Him for a grace so priceless that I cannot, for the life of me, wrap my brain around it. Or get my arms around it. *Still, it's mine. And so I worship.*

Some worry that a preoccupation with God's grace may lead a sinner astray, thinking they have a license to sin. I'd say the exact opposite is true. Jesus Himself said those who have been forgiven much, love much (Luke 7:47). That's certainly been true for me. Every single time after I've blown it and I want to punish myself, I remember the One who took my punishment for me, and my knees buckle. And it makes me—all over again—want to live out my days honoring Him.

What does it mean to "*think about the Lord*"? Let me ask you this question: When you think about someone you deeply love, what comes to mind when you think about him or her?

When I think about my husband, my mind right away goes to his kindness and gentle strength. He's a big guy, mighty in stature; I like that too. He does things with excellence. He doesn't take shortcuts. He loves his family. And the older he gets, the more humbly he relies on his God. I like how his eyebrows and beard are turning gray. I like his sense of humor. And I'm so grateful for how for-me he is.

Think About the Lord

When we think about the Lord, we think about aspects of His character that endear us to Him. Here's what I love about Him: He's mighty in stature and patient and kind. He cares deeply for the poor and the oppressed. He is unchanging, faithful, strong, and true. He is discerning, unwavering, and keeps His Word. He loves humility, hates pride, and refuses to be manipulated. He's content to be misunderstood because He loves His children too much to give in to every selfish whim. He put the stars in place *and* He's numbered the hairs on your head. There's no limit to what He can accomplish and nothing is impossible with

Him. He never looks away, rolls His eyes, or breathes a heavy sigh when your weakness shows. He's protective, invested, and engaged with you every step of the way.

Well, those are just a few of the things I love about Him.

Spend some time thinking about the Lord today. And as you ponder the fact that you serve, and follow, and are related to, a good, good King, remember what it means to be royalty—an heir of God—and joint heir with Christ. His royal blood now runs through your veins. Notice how your prayers take on a new sturdiness and steadfastness when you pray from your God-given place in the heart of God.

I love how Brennan Manning describes God's transformative love:

> Yes, the gracious God enfleshed in Jesus Christ *loves us*. Grace is the active expression of his love. The Christian lives by grace as Abba's child, utterly rejecting the god who catches people by surprise in a sign of weakness—the god incapable of smiling at our awkward mistakes, the god who does not accept a seat at our human festivities, the god who says, 'You will pay for that,' the god incapable of understanding that children will always get dirty and be forgetful, the god always snooping around after sinners . . . Jesus brings *good news* about the Father, not bad news. We need a new kind of relationship with the Father that drives out fear and mistrust and anxiety and guilt, that permits us to be hopeful and joyous, trusting and compassionate. *We have to be converted from the bad news to the good news, from expecting nothing to expecting something.*[1]

We Rely on God's Goodness, Not Ours

When I was a fairly new Christian, I got involved in a young-adults group at my local church. I didn't comfortably know my way around the church building, church politics, or even church lingo, for that matter, and though my heart felt drawn to and at home among Christians, my soul felt unsure and out of place at times.

I'd watch the worship team on stage and marvel at how comfortable they were with the spotlight and with the lyrics. They seemed to know the words to each song instinctively. I imagined they were some of God's favorites because they were so good at what they did and they seemed so established in their faith. From my perspective, I had miles to go before I'd be considered an acceptable Christian.

I still had rough edges around my personality. I didn't own a zipper Bible. I still said things like, "Lordy, this is good ice cream!" not realizing how irreverent I sounded to some. I learned quickly that the playground in elementary school isn't the only place where social hierarchy exists.

Feeling insecure and out of place on a regular basis, I sometimes lingered in the back rows when our large Sunday school class gathered each week. One day in the back row, I met a man who was a tad older than the rest of us. I so wish I could remember his name. He was humble and gentle and reverent when it came to the things of God.

More than once, while leaning forward to take notes on what our speaker had to say that day, I heard a soft mumble coming from my friend beside me. I'd look over and find him with his head bowed, hands folded, and praying under his breath. Then he'd look up, listen for a bit, and then pray some more.

He wasn't well-known in the group. And he was quite easy to miss. But whenever I asked him questions, he smiled at me sweetly, like he enjoyed and appreciated my hunger to learn. He never made me feel inferior or substandard as a Christian. And his insights always compelled me to look up.

Eventually I learned my way around the building, the Bible, and the lingo. I felt more comfortable in my own skin. I got involved in leadership and helped plan events for the hundreds of young adults in our group.

I remember a time at one of our retreats. I arrived early to help with registration, and I stepped into the chapel to see how things were shaping up for the evening session. I stood in the aisle and looked up at the cross and pondered Christ's utter humility and kindness and love; that He would humble Himself to die, even a brutal death on the cross, for sinners who can't fathom just how selfish and sinful we can be.

I was jolted out of my sweet reflective moment when the worship leader brushed past me to take his place on the stage. He walked and talked like a celebrity. Whereas I once thought of him as such a big deal, at that moment, he seemed misled. His big presence and position seemed to upstage the cross on the stage.

Soon the chapel packed in hundreds of young adults. Excitement filled the air. We were all squished in our pews. All of us, that is, except the worship leader. He sat slouched in the front row with his ankle over his knee, his arms stretched along the back of the pew, taking the space of two. He seemed totally disengaged from the service except for when he was up on stage.

I hated that I noticed him, but I couldn't help it, because right next to me was my praying friend. Hidden in the shadows of the retreat chapel with his Bible in his lap and his hands open to heaven, he reverently bowed his head. I knew he was praying for every soul in the room, that we'd all encounter God and know His love even more deeply than the week before.

The contrast of these two souls staggered me. I couldn't help myself. I looked back and forth between them, one hidden and intimately connecting to God, and the other under the spotlight and loving every minute of it. I felt a new and holy fear of God settle into my soul.

Not to say that every single person in the spotlight has the celebrity syndrome. Some are called to that place, and those who serve with humble reverence have paid a significant price to stay the course and give God the glory He deserves. Pray for those precious brothers and sisters. And it's not to say that those with hidden ministries never deal with ambition, or frustration, or jealousy. That's why we need to pray for each other, because we all have our trials and temptations.

But the point is, we must never stop relying on God's goodness. He is the One who paid for our place at the table of grace.

When life is good, we sometimes forget *why* we're heirs.

Maybe you don't go to the beggar table when you blow it. Good for you for remembering who you are! I need a good reminder every once in a while because I suffer from my own occasional bouts of "heir amnesia." For many if not most of us, we need to remember that we're heirs, even in times of despair.

Just as important, we must remember why we're heirs. The truth is, when you and I walk faithfully with God, when we take Him at His Word, when we believe His promises and pray like we mean it, over time we'll see changes in our circumstances, fruit in our lives, and redemption in our perspectives. And the temptation will be to think that we had something to do with all of the glory and grace evident in our lives.

Picture yourself sitting at the heir table. You're comfortable there. Suddenly, a meek and mild woman, new to the faith, approaches you and notices the life of abundance you enjoy. She asks, "How did you get there?"

It's tempting to polish your nails with your breath, rub them on your chest, and proceed to tell her about all of your disciplines and formulas (okay, I know I'm overstating here, but bear with me for the sake of the point). You look up at her gladly, and a bit proudly, and say, "Well, I'm here because I do devotions every morning (*well, most of the time*). And I serve on five committees at church (*but I'm exhausted*). I give lots away (*most of the time*). And I don't gossip (*much*). And if you do all of the good things I do, one day you'll be as amazing as I am." (Smile.)

I purposely painted a caricature so we can more clearly see how it looks when we take any kind of credit whatsoever for our privileged heir status. If we weren't in Christ, we wouldn't have the right to such an inheritance. Amazing grace, how can it be? Not one of us can boast about the unmerited, beautiful gift of grace. We didn't earn a speck of it.

But because of this great gift, we are now royalty. And grasping such a truth should inspire only humble gratitude. Never pride or judgment.

Here's a quick word for both the new Christian who feels out of sorts and out of place, and for the seasoned Christian who knows her way around her church and her Bible:

If you know your way around your church and your Bible, praise God! But do understand if you're a seasoned Christian, you're not more valuable to man or less accountable before God just because you've been here awhile.

Grasping the truth of our heir status should never inspire pride or judgment. Only humble gratitude.

And if you're new to the faith and feel awkward because you aren't familiar with the lingo or the language yet, know this: *You have as much right to be here as the rest of us, and you're every bit as valuable to God as any one of us. And every bit as saved.*

God is always good and is always good to us, even when we can't always discern His hand in our lives. But here's the thing: Just because He's always good to us, doesn't mean He's always good with everything we do.

Consider the Israelites. They followed a miraculous cloud by day and a pillar of fire by night. They passed through the sea on dry ground and ate fresh manna from heaven each and every day. God was good to them. But He was not pleased *with* them. Read on:

> For I do not want you to be unaware, brothers, that our fathers were all under the cloud, and all passed through the sea, and all were baptized into Moses in the cloud and in the sea, and all ate the same spiritual food, and all drank the same spiritual drink. For they drank from the spiritual Rock that followed them, and the Rock was Christ. Nevertheless, with most of them God was not pleased, for they were overthrown in the wilderness.
>
> 1 Corinthians 10:1–5 ESV

We can lose our way and our footing in a heartbeat the minute we think life is good because we're good, or that God owes us when life gets uncomfortable. Dr. Warren Wiersbe writes:

> Privilege is not a guarantee of success. . . . there are dangers to maturity as well as to immaturity, and one of them is over-confidence. When we think we are strong, we discover that we are weak. . . . Good beginnings do not guarantee good endings. . . . Experience must be balanced with caution, for we never come to a place in our Christian walk where we are free from temptation and failure. . . . Yet, God provides a way for us to overcome.[2]

We do well to learn from those who've gone before us. God miraculously provided for His people. He's so invested in our journey. And yet the Israelites, like us sometimes, were bent toward idolatry, immorality, irreverence, and irritation. And God was not pleased with them.

Their story serves as a cautionary word for us. The minute we think we can stand on our past Christian laurels, our vast Christian experience, or our impressive Christian résumé, or that we can stomp our feet and demand anything from God (or people, for that matter), we need to take heed and remember why we stand and why we are heirs, lest we fall.

> Now these things happened to them as an example, but they were written down for our instruction, on whom the end of the ages has come. Therefore let anyone who thinks that he stands take heed lest he fall. No temptation has overtaken you that is not common to man. God is faithful, and he will not let you be tempted beyond your ability, but with the temptation he will also provide the way of escape, that you may be able to endure it.
>
> 1 Corinthians 10:11–13 ESV

If we stay humbly grateful, we will be powerful in prayer and protected from the self-sins that threaten to derail us. If the Spirit of God convicts us for our wandering ways, we're wise to humbly respond and thank Jesus for His mercy and grace. But when the enemy condemns us for those same missteps, we can turn a deaf ear to our accuser and listen instead to the Father's song over our lives. Can you hear it?

> *You are My beloved one. You are forgiven and you are free.*
> *I am yours and you are Mine.*
> *Nothing and no one will ever snatch you from My hand.*
> *You get to be a work in progress without the condemnation.*
> *It is for freedom that I set you free.*
> *Refuse to subject yourself to the lying voice of the enemy.*
> *Because of My victory in your life, he has lost the right to*
>   *accuse you.*
> *You are free to become all I've promised you would be!*
> *Let's enjoy this journey together. I've got you and you've*
>   *got Me.*

God is good. His promises are true. And He will always make a way for us.

A Blessing for You

May you refuse condemnation for the ways you fail and fall short in your everyday life. May you instead embrace God's relentless grace that covers you from head to toe. May others' opinions no longer tie you up in knots, because God's opinion continually sets you free! May you determine—with all your heart—to live the abundant, powerful, forgiven life Jesus has offered you. Lean in to the soul-stirring, heart-freeing grace that Jesus purchased just for you. Rest fully assured today that Jesus has you close to His heart.

Let's Pray . . .

Precious Jesus, I bow humbly before You and open my hands. Fill me once again with a fresh revelation of Your great love. Awaken me to the reality of Your unrelenting goodness. Teach me more about Your kindness. I'm learning that the more I rely on Your goodness, the more sturdy my steps become. The more I trust in Your grace, the more powerfully I dare to pray. I've much to learn about Your power and Your promises, but I want to learn! So teach me, Lord. Help me to rest and rely on the supernatural grace You've imparted to me. Help me to see myself as the heir You've made me to be. When You search the world over for those with faith and humility, may You find these things in me. In Jesus' name, I pray, Amen.

Praying God's Word

Write out a personalized prayer and weave in the truths of the following Scripture. Make the declaration that no matter what you're facing right now, nothing can separate you from the love of God!

> This is love: not that we loved God, but that he loved us and sent his Son as an atoning sacrifice for our sins.
>
> 1 John 4:10

_____

_____

_____

_____

A POWERFUL WORD: *You Are Worthy*

We can't outrun ourselves. Our untended heart will spill out in ways we had not meant it to. We are invited to enter green pastures of goodness and mercy, for it's in the presence of Christ and under his tutelage that we are assured of our worth.[3]

Personal Reflection

1. Do you tend to keep a mental record of the good things you've done, or the not-so-good things? Why do you suppose that is?

2. Recall a time when God's goodness trumped your badness and you felt overwhelmed by His kindness. How did that experience impact your prayers during that season?

3. In what circumstances do you tend to "loosen your grip on grace" because you feel confident in your own ability? What do your prayers sound like in those situations?

4. In what circumstances do you find yourself utterly dependent on God's grace, goodness, and provision?

5. Picture yourself a year from now. Imagine yourself with a new freedom in Christ and a new awareness of what He's done for you. Describe the new and empowered you.

6. What has to change in your life *now* so you can walk in the kind of freedom you described above?

7. Spend some time in prayer and thank God for His goodness. Ask Him to give you a proper perspective regarding the importance of your obedience *and* the power of His grace. His grace saves and empowers us to obey. The more we rely on His grace, the more sincerely obedient we will be.

Group Reflection

1. Share about a time you observed someone who seemed to humbly and gratefully understand grace.

2. How does our understanding of God's goodness (versus our ability) affect our prayers?

3. When has God's grace felt believable and tangible to you? Can you share the circumstances surrounding that time?

4. Consider the passage from 1 Corinthians 10 again and talk about how the Israelites' missteps could just as easily be our missteps. Look at the sins recorded in this passage (idolatry, immorality, irreverence, and irritation). How might those translate today?

5. Just because God is good to us doesn't mean He's good with everything we do. Talk about the importance of our choices and attitudes, not for the sake of earning our status, but for the sake of obedience to God and power in our prayers.

6. How has your understanding of grace evolved over the years?

7. In 2 Corinthians 9, we read about God's ability to help us abound in every good work. What's the catalyst? It's grace. God's grace enables us to *abound*, which means to thrive, prosper, and overflow with more than enough. How does grace allow such a miracle of multiplication in our lives? Take your best guess.

7

Dare to Pray God's Promises

You're Anchored

I believe there is a God in heaven who directs our steps, who prepares good works in advance, who causes all things to work together for the good, who fights our battles for us! And if you pray through, there will be a breakthrough! Don't lose heart. Don't lose hope. Don't lose faith. Don't lose patience.

Mark Batterson, *Draw the Circle*

If you remain in Me and My words remain in you [that is, if we are vitally united and My message lives in your heart], ask whatever you wish and it will be done for you. My Father is glorified and honored by this, when you bear much fruit, and prove yourselves to be My [true] disciples.

John 15:7–8 AMP

Recently I interviewed author and pastor Adonis Lenzy about the importance of taking the next steps God has for us. Adonis talked about how often we wait on God when He's actually the one waiting on us. And yet, Adonis implored, we have to be people who develop a lifestyle of listening to God so we know what our next steps should be. Adonis expressed how deeply his grandmother inspired him in this regard. She loved God's Word, prayed passionately, and spent a whole lot of time listening for what God had to say. Adonis talked about his grandma, and I couldn't help but picture Miss Clara from the film *War Room*. (If you haven't seen that movie, can I just say? You must!)

Adonis said his grandma practiced "knee-ology." She developed her theology from time spent in God's Word and from the countless hours she spent on her knees. One day after a particularly powerful time with the Lord, she met up with her girlfriends for lunch. She shared some of the amazing things God had shown her and even inspired her to believe Him for.

Her friends giggled a bit and questioned if she really heard those things from God. I'm guessing they were wild, audacious kinds of things. I love those kinds of prayers.

This dear woman of God leaned in and said these bold words to her friends: *I love you, girls, but I must say, I've been walking with the Lord too long to take your word over His.*[1] Loved this!

Though it's important to be open to counsel and feedback from our friends and loved ones, sometimes God's words to us will defy logic. Sometimes God invites us to a faith that calls us to seemingly stand alone. But we're never alone. We're always anchored to Him. It's especially during such times that we must trust God with everything in us and take only the next steps He lays out for us.

> Trust in the LORD with all your heart
> and lean not on your own understanding;
> in all your ways submit to him,
> and he will make your paths straight.
> Proverbs 3:5–6

I can echo Adonis's grandmother's words. The more I read God's Word and the more I seek His face, the more familiar I am with His voice. Furthermore, the more clearly I hear Him and recognize His direction in my life, the more I dare ask Him to accomplish things only He can accomplish and the less I tend to rely on the limited view of my own perspective during that time in between.

Here's a short list from the long list of things I've prayed for over the years. And though I'm still praying and waiting to see a breakthrough in certain circumstances, God has answered some of my prayers in ways I never could have fathomed:

- I prayed passionately and consistently for God to heal my soul, to make me whole, and to help me grasp the worth I have in Him. Though I still have my moments of uncertainty and insecurity, I now walk in holy confidence and humble dependence with great consistency. *So grateful to You, Lord!*

- I prayed persistently and consistently about my health, and so strongly sensed God had more to do with me, in me, and through me. I've mostly recovered from Lyme disease. Though I still have health challenges, I am physically strong and healthy and can get a lot done in a day. *Thank You, Lord!*

- I grabbed hold of certain promises regarding my husband's job and I refused to let go; I knew my prayers lined up with God's will. In due time, God broke through in the most marvelous way (I tell the story in chapter 10). Kev adds great value to his company, and this job has completely changed our family and faith dynamics. *So very grateful!*

- I believed strongly God called me to write (even though I still have such a long way to go when it comes to the craft). I prayed, attended writers' conferences, wrote, and prayed some more. I worked like everything depended on me and prayed like it all depended on God. In due season, His direct call on my life came to fruition. This God-given dream came true. *So very grateful. Thank You, Lord.*

- I knew in my soul that God called Kevin and me to be generous givers, especially to ministries that care for the poor. Yet our finances were a mess. So I grabbed hold of God for everything I was worth. I prayed His promises. We repented of our unbelief and inconsistency. We applied God's principles to our finances. We engaged our faith. And we gradually increased our giving. To this day, we continue to receive fresh vision for what God wants to do in and through us financially. The enemy's plan for our finances has been blown to smithereens. We are conduits to God's kingdom work on the earth today. *Praise!*

- I spent many days and nights facedown before the Lord, appealing Him to draw my sons back to Him. Not that they'd rejected their faith, but they walked in the ways of the world for a time. Still, my husband and I hadn't raised them to blend in with the world. God has moved and continues to move in their hearts and ours; He's working all things together for our good and His glory. We're eternally grateful. *Thank You, Jesus.*

- I pray regularly for missionaries, the military, and their families. I ask God to perform miracles in their midst. And my heart is stirred every time I read stories of God's intervention! *And so I continue to pray consistently and earnestly.*

- I continue to pray for the lukewarm state of the church and for the persecuted church. We desperately need a revival in this land and elsewhere. *And so I continue to passionately and persistently pray.*

God's Attention to Detail

I'm overwhelmed by God's goodness and His attention to detail. Looking back, I can clearly see His wisdom in making me wait for the desperate desires of my heart. I can also see why He invited me to be a part of certain solutions, one faith step at a time. God's involvement and His call for my engagement showed me time and time again how deeply He wants to partner with us to accomplish His purposes on earth.

He truly works all things together for the good of those who love Him and are called according to His purpose (Romans 8:28). And He's not slow to act, as if He's somehow incapable of moving fast. Rather, His answers take time because He works through people, and so often *we* are the ones who are slow to respond!

I now know this with all my heart: My prayers over the years *have* impacted things on earth, and those same prayers have utterly changed *me*.

My hope in Jesus has only grown with time. My handle on His promises is firmer now than in years past. My capacity to understand His love has grown exponentially in battle. I've learned that though we endure trials and hardships and not-yet seasons, we *will* overcome because Jesus already overcame.

I'll tell you, for me, having to appeal to God in heaven for each of these "not-yets," having to battle the doubt and fear and unbelief, having to silence the enemy's taunts and threats, having to grab hold of God's promises and not let go, and then having to *wait* on God for the answers to my prayers, well, honestly, this process has been hard on my perspective at times. But more important, this same battle has absolutely transformed my soul.

Read this passage and picture it, if you can:

> So God has given both his promise and his oath. These two things are unchangeable because it is impossible for God to lie.

Therefore, we who have fled to him for refuge can have great confidence as we hold to the hope that lies before us. This hope is a strong and trustworthy anchor for our souls. It leads us through the curtain into God's inner sanctuary.

Hebrews 6:18–19 NLT

The thing about an anchor is that it's built to withstand the fiercest of storms. An anchor worth its weight will hold no matter which way the winds are blowing.

You and I are anchored upward to God, where He sits on His throne in His inner sanctuary. Imagine that! And though the storms rage and the winds just about knock us over, we're anchored to God Almighty. And no person, circumstance, storm, or enemy scheme can keep us from His love and faithfulness.

Picture your soul's anchor leading upward. Remember that God's hold on you is stronger than your hold on Him. He's relying on Himself (not you) to get you safely home. This is not to say that your choices don't matter. Just the opposite is true. You are here on this earth to walk intimately with God and to partner with Him to accomplish His purposes on earth.

You will have to fight for some of the things He's promised you. You will have to stand on His Word even when it doesn't feel true. But the battle will be worth it. And when it's all over but the shouting, you can be assured that Jesus will get you safely home, because that's exactly what He promised He'd do.

Having to contend for the things that God puts on my heart while the enemy works to steal my joy, kill my dreams, and destroy my sense of purpose—well, this fight has made me a fiercer woman of prayer. Anything worth having is worth praying for.

Because of Christ and our faith in him, we can now come boldly and confidently into God's presence.

Ephesians 3:12 NLT

Persevering Prayer

Prayer takes perseverance and perspective. Prayer requires sensitivity to the Holy Spirit and strategy from God's Word. Standing strong and praying through those times-in-between calls for holy grit and God's abundant grace.

If prayer were easy, everyone would do it. But those who've learned the secret of intimacy with God, who've gotten ahold of God's promises for themselves, there's no stopping them. They now know there's no better use of their time, no greater impact they can make, and no deeper well they can draw from than the one they've found in Christ Jesus.

Standing strong and praying through those times-in-between calls for holy grit and God's abundant grace.

He's our Lord of Hosts, Captain of God's army. We're most powerful when we pray and most influential when we're in step with almighty God.

Heir Promises

Here are some of the promises that anchored me to Christ when my circumstances threatened to either turn me upside down or at least tempt me to doubt that God would come through for me. May you shift your weight onto these promises and may they strengthen your own soul today.[2]

> So do not fear, for I am with you; do not be dismayed, for I am your God. I will strengthen you and help you; I will uphold you with my righteous right hand.
>
> Isaiah 41:10

Those who sow with tears will reap with songs of joy. Those who go out weeping, carrying seed to sow, will return with songs of joy, carrying sheaves with them.

Psalm 126:5–6

I remain confident of this: I will see the goodness of the LORD in the land of the living.

Psalm 27:13

Give, and it will be given to you. A good measure, pressed down, shaken together and running over, will be poured into your lap. For with the measure you use, it will be measured to you.

Luke 6:38

This is the confidence we have in approaching God: that if we ask anything according to his will, he hears us. And if we know that he hears us—whatever we ask—we know that we have what we asked of him.

1 John 5:14–15

Take delight in the LORD, and he will give you the desires of your heart.

Psalm 37:4

"Truly I tell you, if you have faith as small as a mustard seed, you can say to this mountain, 'Move from here to there,' and it will move. Nothing will be impossible for you."

Matthew 17:20

I've learned that it's impossible for God to fail me. And it's impossible for God to fail you. It is, however, completely possible, plausible, and probable for God *not* to give us what we want when we want it. And such times test and prove our faith.

But as a loving, invested Father whose heart and character are tethered to His Word, it's impossible for Him to do anything other than what He said He would do. God's promises are absolutely true. They're not dusty or old. They've not diminished over time. They are as potent and powerful as they've ever been. And so we pray with passion and boldness, humility and faith.

> How things appear to us, and how they actually are, are rarely the same. Sometimes it *looks* and *feels* like the Almighty is dealing "very bitterly" with us, when all the while he is doing us and many others more good than we can imagine. God's purposes in the lives of his children are *always* gracious. Always. If they don't look like it, don't trust your perceptions. Trust God's promises. He is *always* filling His promises.[3]

> Let us seize and hold tightly the confession of our hope without wavering, for He who promised is reliable and trustworthy and faithful [to His word].

> Hebrews 10:23 AMP

Rely on His Promises

We're most powerful in prayer when we pray God's Word and rely on His promises. We have access and invitation to pray God's Word over the very situations that burden our hearts. And this process of petition, persistence, and perseverance, it transforms us as we go. So not only do we get to partner with God to see things change on this earth, He partners with us so that we're changed from the inside out. When we as His people trust Him and do what He says, He makes sure we are forever changed (by His grace and for His glory) after the trials and the battles we walk through. God is brilliant that way.

God's promises are as potent and powerful as they've ever been.

113

When we wait long for a breakthrough, we tend to forget that even here, right in our everyday moments, spiritual activity swirls all around us. We can't see it, can't always feel it, but sometimes we can perceive it.

If we'll lean in and listen for the Lord's voice, and if we look for Him more than we do the answers we so desire, God will sometimes offer glimpses of what He is up to in us and around us. He'll fine-tune our focus to see the little sprouts springing from the ground, or the trickle of a stream in the wasteland, or the fist-sized cloud in the sky, or the subtle shift in attitude in the heart of one of our loved ones.

God *is* doing a new thing. Can you perceive it? Can you sense it? If you've gone too long without seeing the sun and you find yourself wondering if God cares at all and if His promises are worth their weight to you, then it's time to look back over your shoulder at the road you've taken and remember the goodness of God. Then may you lean in, cup your ear, and listen for God's gentle whisper and divine direction. He'll point you to evidences of His goodness right in your midst.

God is doing a new thing.

Can you perceive it?

Can you sense it?

He Is Who He Says He Is

When John the Baptist sat in prison, most likely knowing the fate that awaited him, he battled his own bout of discouragement and doubt. Imagine, one of the greatest men who ever lived, according to Jesus, yet his heart and soul were weary and in need of a reminder that Jesus was who He said He was.

John sent word to Jesus' disciples asking if He indeed was the Messiah or if they should keep looking for someone else. Jesus answered this way:

"Go and tell John the things you have seen and heard: that the blind see, the lame walk, the lepers are cleansed, the deaf hear, the dead are raised, the poor have the gospel preached to them. And blessed is he who is not offended because of Me."[4]

Three things stand out to me here. When we get weary in the waiting, we're at risk of loosening our grip on God's promises because . . .

- We forget about God's past faithfulness
- We doubt God's *current* activity in our midst
- We blame Him for our troubles

Jesus' answer to John's question seems filled with compassion and mixed with a bit of caution. When we reside in that time in-between, it's common for us to be so focused on the angst in our heart and on the unmet desires in our lives that we forget that God has never failed us in the past. And He has always come through at just the right time.

If you find yourself in one such season, step away from your current situation and recount again some of the ways that God has come through for you. Declare right now, that though you can't see it, God is at work in your midst. He moves when you pray and He absolutely cherishes your faith. Believe it. Embrace it. Because it's true.

And if you're tempted to blame God for your current hardship, I encourage you to consider this a dead-end attitude, one that will derail your faith and perspective. Why blame the very One who can do something about your circumstances?

Nobody loves you like God. Nobody keeps his or her promises like God does. And nobody has the wisdom to intervene at just the right time like God does, and like God will.

Jesus says that we're blessed when—even amidst really difficult circumstances in life—we choose not to blame Him or be offended by what He allows us to endure. Think about what He endured: torture, persecution, rejection. Yet Jesus never got offended with His Father, even when He turned His face away. How's that possible?

It's possible when you believe that the heart of your Father is *always* good, and that anything He allows you to endure will serve you and glorify Him in the end.

Trust His process. Trust His promises. He knows what He's doing with your life. Pray passionately. Speak precisely. Keep believing. Keep walking. Rest when He tells you to. Stand in faith. Embrace courage.

We have His Word. We have His presence. We have His promises. We have everything we need to live a powerful kingdom life.

> His divine power has given us everything we need for a godly life through our knowledge of him who called us by his own glory and goodness.
>
> 2 Peter 1:3

A Blessing for You

May new and fresh hope suddenly arise within you. May the enemy's plan against you backfire as you grow stronger, not weaker, in your trials. May your sturdy grasp of God's promises intimidate the enemy and make him lose heart. May you find JOY in the heat of the battle, POWER in the promises of God, and PROVISION where you've known lack. May the things you once knew of God pale in comparison to what you know of Him now. He makes all things new. He breaks through. And He will come through for you. Soldier on, mighty one! God is with you!

Let's Pray . . .

Precious Lord, where do I begin? You've been so good to me. And though I may not see it at the moment, You are being good to me in this place while I wait for a breakthrough. I know that You will continue to look after that which concerns me. Draw me ever closer to You. Take my prayers and make them powerful. Help me to take Your promises and make them mine. I want to be mighty in prayer and ferocious in faith. Open my eyes to see the ways You're working in my midst. Give me a sense of Your heart for me and for the things that concern me. Show me promises from Your word that are mine for the taking. Help me to stand on Your word and not move until my eyes see what my heart already knows: You are faithful and true and I belong to You. How blessed I am! Thank You, dear Jesus, Amen.

Praying God's Word

Write out a personalized prayer and weave in the truths of the following Scripture. Make the declaration that no matter what you're facing right now, nothing can separate you from the love of God!

Because he turned his ear to me, I will call on him as long as I live.

Psalm 116:2

_____

_____

_____

_____

A POWERFUL WORD: *Our Faith Honors God*

Audacious faith dares to believe the Word and claim friendship with God. We do God more honor by believing what He has said about Himself and having the courage to come boldly to the throne of grace than by hiding in self-conscious humility among the trees of the garden.[5]

Personal Reflection

1. What are the top five concerns of your heart?
2. Do you have promises from Scripture that you stand on and pray from? List those verses if you have them.
3. Think back to when you first started praying about these issues. Have you seen any breakthrough, any movement, any answer to prayer? Write down your thoughts.
4. Look back on the other times when God took longer than you'd hoped to bring an answer. What takeaways or benefits are now yours as a result? How did those battles change you?
5. Consider the difference between rote repetition and earnest supplication in your prayer life. One is a recipe for disengagement while the other is a catalyst to spiritual traction. Which of these most describes the consistent cries of your heart? Are you going through the motions or are you grabbing hold of something in God while you wait for your breakthrough?
6. If you find yourself going through the motions, spend time just seeking God for who He is. Ask Him to breathe fresh wind into your sails. If you're fully engaged but weary, ask Him to do the same. Keep on keeping on.
7. What do you sense God is saying to you today regarding the desires of your heart? Lean in and listen, then write down your thoughts.

Group Reflection

1. Share about one of your greatest prayer battles, including the prayer, the time in-between, and the outcome.

2. How are you different as a result of that battle?

3. What did you learn about yourself, about God, and about prayer from that experience?

4. Share about a time when things didn't turn out the way you'd hoped. What did you learn about God and about prayer from that experience?

5. Share in your own words why Jesus so intimately connects abiding in Him with powerful prayer. (Revisit the opening verse: John 15:7–8.)

6. Give your thoughts on the difference between rote repetition and earnest supplication in prayer. Will God answer your prayers if your heart is disengaged? I think He does, sometimes. But what's the difference between rote versus earnest prayer?

7. How can you keep your prayer life alive and active (so you don't fall into the habit of going through the motions)?

8

Dare to Pray From Victory

You're a Warrior

The kingdom of God is never in trouble, the kingdom of God never runs out of resources and the kingdom of God is never lacking in power. Therefore, those who live with God in this available kingdom are never in trouble, never lack provision, and never lack power. In the kingdom of God, I discover that I am safe, significant, and strong.

> Dallas Willard, paraphrased by James Bryan Smith,
> *Eternal Living*

Can anything ever separate us from Christ's love? Does it mean he no longer loves us if we have trouble or calamity, or are persecuted, or hungry, or destitute, or in danger, or threatened with death? . . . No, despite all these things, overwhelming victory is ours through Christ, who loved us.

> Romans 8:35, 37 NLT

The light turned green, but the car ahead of me didn't budge. Cars lined up behind me ready to drive through the intersection. It was our turn, after all. But the guy in front of me stayed put. I waited for what felt like a respectable amount of time and then gave a quick tap of my horn.

Big mistake.

The driver moved forward a few feet, then suddenly slammed on his brakes. I came to a screeching halt in the middle of the intersection. The yellow light turned red. The drivers on my left and right inched forward and waited for me and for the other guy to get out of the intersection because it was now their turn to go. I peeked in my rearview mirror at my three little ones in the car with me, all buckled in their car seats. I swallowed hard.

The driver pulled ahead again, just enough for me to move through the intersection. But once he got up to the speed limit he hit his brakes. Again I slammed on my brakes and my kids' little heads whipped forward and then back. They shouted out, "What's happening, Momma?"

Crazy driver man did this over and over again. He clearly intended to send me a message. I moved to the other lane and tried to move past him, but he'd have none of it. He pulled in front of me and repeatedly accelerated and then hit his brakes. Then he pulled next to me really close, opened his window, screamed out his window, and laid on the horn with one long, steady blare.

I anxiously prayed, kept my eyes fixed straight ahead, and stayed focused on the road ahead of me even though I had a rage-aholic next to me.

My little ones stretched their necks and looked out the window at the man whose fury was focused on us. One of them said, "Momma, he's making a gun out of his fingers and aiming at us like he's gonna shoot us." Ugh! I gripped my steering wheel and as calmly as I could, replied, "Kids, don't look at him; he's only trying to scare you. Look straight ahead, out my front window, so you can see where we're going."

The crazy man followed me for miles. He alternately pulled ahead of me, hit his brakes, and then pulled beside me and laid on his horn. I never saw his face because I refused even to look his way. I didn't want to remember him and I didn't want him to see the fear in my eyes. I prayed and focused and looked straight ahead. Eventually I came upon a police officer whose presence motivated the crazy man to back off and drive like a normal person.

Recently, as I've walked through various battles, I've heard God's gentle whisper across my heart, "Though the enemy has you in his crosshairs, don't look at him; *don't look at the shooter.* Tune him out and look at Me. Fix your eyes straight ahead. I'll get you to where you need to go."

Without realizing it, our gaze often pulls to the object of our fears, don't you think? We listen to the enemy's taunts and threats, and we freeze in our tracks. And we stare at the fears in front of us until they actually get *in* us. The enemy likes it that way. His greatest war tactic is to scare us (or distract us or discourage us) to such a degree that we forget who we are. Because, when we rise up in Christ's authority and we entrust ourselves to *His* care, well, we become downright dangerous. And that enemy? He gets put in his place. Under our feet.

Without realizing it, our gaze often pulls to the object of our fears.

> I've given you true authority. You can smash vipers and scorpions under your feet. You can walk all over the power of the enemy. You can't be harmed.
>
> Luke 10:19 THE VOICE

Focus and Fight Like You Can Win

Several times in my book *Your Sacred Yes*, I referenced a time in my life after my dad died—a period when I walked through a dark night of the soul. My heart felt broken for so many reasons. I missed my dad. Wished I had visited him more. Also, I was done raising my sons. They were all grown up. My house was empty and my heart felt the same. And two of my sons took paths so different than I envisioned, different than I had trained them for. Still, we enjoyed great times with our kids and belly-laughed until our faces hurt. But my heart hurt too.

The enemy's lie to me during that time was this: *None of what you taught your kids stuck. They are more acquainted with your generational sins than they are with your spiritual roots. And there's* nothing *you can do about it.*

And I was tempted to believe this lie. Because it certainly felt true.

And honestly, some of my grief was a mid-life thing. I grieved over how gravity was winning the day in my body. I grieved over how many new wrinkles appeared on my face without my permission. And I grieved over the fact that I couldn't seem to get out from under the blanket of spiritual oppression that the enemy wrapped around my head. I couldn't breathe, couldn't see, and just could not find my footing.

One particular day I curled up in a ball and cried. I felt only defeat and discouragement. My husband didn't know what to do with me, bless his heart. He finally sat down next to me and spoke words that I'll not soon forget. With strength and conviction he challenged me, "Why don't you fight this battle like you fight every other battle? You're *not* done fighting for our kids. And the enemy doesn't get to keep taunting you this way. Don't you remember who you are? Whose you are? It's time to get up and fight."

And he was right. I'd lost my footing because I'd lost my focus. I felt like my little boys must have felt that day years ago when they—buckled in the back seat—looked out the window at the scary guy who threatened to shoot them. I felt stuck at the mercy of my enemy, and with no defense. Like I was strapped to a chair and forced to listen to the threats and rage of someone whose only aim was to destroy me. Only you can't really turn your hand into a gun, and the enemy can't really turn a lie into a truth no matter how big he gets in the face of our fears.

Something rose up within me after my husband's pep talk and I remembered once again who I was and Whose I was. Though there were no cameras in my house to capture the scene, I will say that my comeback play closely resembled the epic moment in the film *War Room* when Elizabeth decided to put the devil in his place. Here's a peek at her battle-stance moment when she gave that enemy a piece of her mind:

> I don't know where you are, devil, but I know you can hear me. . . . You have played with my mind. And had your way long enough. No more! You are done! Jesus is Lord of this house, and that means there's no place for you anymore! So take your lies, your schemes, your accusations, and get out! In Jesus' name! You can't have my marriage, you can't have my daughter, and you sure can't have my man! This house is under new management, and that means you are out![1]

C'mon, somebody! Doesn't her declaration just put a fire in your belly? There's something powerful about rising up in the strength of the Lord and declaring to your soul and to your enemy that *Jesus* is your strong tower, your shelter against the foe, your defender, deliverer, and mighty God! His strength and power inhabits your soul! You have Him! You have His power. And you have His promises.

How could I have forgotten these precious truths in the face of such heartache? Well, things changed for me after that day. I started to pray with precision and power. I would not be denied. The more I prayed God's promises, the more assurance, strength, and clarity fueled my passion and my prayers.

I can say this for sure: I am better for this battle. In fact, I'm forever grateful that God allowed me to walk through that valley. I have a new resolve to stand strong; a new understanding of my authority in Him; and a new compassion for parents whose hearts are broken over some of the choices their kids have made. I now pray bigger prayers with bigger faith and a broader perspective. When I pray for the desires of my heart, I also pray for the many, like me, who long for the same things I do.

And guess what? My kids walked through their own storms, faced down their own battles, and you know what happened? When the elements raged against them, their own spiritual root systems activated, like God always knew they would. He was never worried about my kids. Our sons have found their way back home again. Or should I say, Jesus kept a close eye on them and when the time was right, wooed them back to a close relationship with Him. The enemy lied. My kids have spiritual roots that are stronger than my generational sins. Thank You, Lord!

I'm overwhelmed with thanksgiving and amazed at the preciseness with which Jesus has answered some of my very specific prayers for my kids.

We've had countless deep discussions with our sons about their long journey home. I treasure their insights and their honesty about their questions and their struggles. It makes me respect them all the more. Their sinful bent pulled them toward worldliness and their integrity compelled them to wrestle with life and truth in a way that was real to them. And you know? We're all better from having traveled this journey. Because we have a story to tell.

We all have our battles. Without them we'd be weak-kneed saints who too quickly lose our footing. Trials train us to stand. Battles teach us how to fight. And God's promises remind us of what's true about us and about God. And isn't it something how when we've come through hard times and have learned how to stand and fight and pray amidst those trials, that we're able to declare with even greater assurance that God is on our side and that nothing is too difficult for Him?

> If there weren't a wall standing in your way today, how would you be able to give glory to God for the victory He wants to give you in the future? How would you be able to praise God in the sight of your friends and neighbors for providing for you, healing you, forgiving you, giving you grace, or coming through for you in the nick of time? . . . Unless we had trials and obstacles to defeat, what other opportunity would we have to cultivate our character and increase our faith? [2]

Heir Privileges

The truth of the matter is, as heirs of God and joint heirs with Christ, we have certain privileges. We have His presence, His promises, and His power. *Let that sink in for a moment.* In fact, let me say it again: We have His presence—His holy, awe-inspiring presence where the fullness of joy is found. We have His promises—His faithful, true promises that change everything for the Christ-follower. And we have His power—the same power that raised Christ from the dead, available to us. We're more spiritual than physical, more found than lost, and more loved than we know. Isn't that just something?

And though we face giants who aim to destroy us, and an enemy who's always in a bad mood, we serve a joy-filled, patient, kind, and loving Father who always leads us triumphantly through our battles.

We're on an upward journey to the Holy City. Heaven will be wonderful. No more tears. No more heartache. No more sickness. No more disease. No more loss. Imagine. But we're not there yet. We're still here on earth for a reason. And Jesus hasn't left us ill-equipped or unprepared.

We're more spiritual than physical, more found than lost, and more loved than we know.

Max Lucado joined me recently on my radio show to talk about his fantastic book *Glory Days*. I always love talking with this gifted, gentle, humble man of God. I got especially excited when I read these words from the book's promotional material. Take a deep breath and be encouraged today. Though you and I may feel beat up by life at times, we'll win more than we lose, and when it's all said and done, we'll still be standing.

> Promised Land people choose to trust God's promises. They choose to believe that God is up to something good even though all we see looks bad. . . . You were not made to quake in fear. You were not made to be beholden to your past. You were not made to limp through life as a wimp. You are a living, breathing expression of God. What's more, He fights for you. The big news of the Bible is not that you fight for God, but that God fights for you. And to know this—to know that your Father fights for you—is an unparalleled source of empowerment. This is your inheritance: more victory than defeat, more joy than sadness, more hope than despair . . . You'll always face problems. But you don't have to face them in the same way. Instead, immerse your mind in God-thoughts. Turn a deaf ear to doubters. Set your mind on a holy cause. Once you find your mountain, no giant will stop you, no age will disqualify you, no problems will defeat you.[3]

It's time to reframe our disappointments in light of God's promises. It's time to face our battles with courage in light of

God's power. And it's time to pray with passion and precision because Jesus truly *hears us* when we pray. He promises that the prayers of His people will accomplish great and powerful things.

Let's take our stand and declare Jesus' name over every one of our battles. We will not be shaken. We will not be defeated. We will not be derailed from the kingdom life God has promised us. Every battle we face will serve us well in the end because we serve a God who fights for us. He uses our hardships to teach us what's true about our inheritance in Him.

And this Warrior King? He loves us beyond anything our minds can comprehend. We're blessed. We're loved. We're victors.

Owen Strachan, author of *Risky Gospel*, writes:

> We have a great task before us, but we have even greater power working in us. Our central encouragement is this: God doesn't leave us alone. He calls us to a great mission, offers us tremendous adventure, but then surprises us by telling us that He will be right beside us. He's always worked that way. . . . God doesn't want His people to be fearful, but faithful. He's not trying to cool us down, but to heat us up. Yet, biblical faith isn't reckless or careless. It is trusting, confident, and fearless because it's grounded in Almighty God.[4]

We choose our perspective. We decide if we're going to worship or whine. We're the ones who get to embrace faith and courage. And we're the ones God rewards when it's all said and done. This battle you're facing? It's a perfect opportunity to engage your faith, to develop perseverance, to mature your perspective, and to remember God's love. Walk forward in faith. You have every reason to trust Him.

A Blessing for You

As you step back and survey the parts of your life that break your heart or that don't make sense right now, may you dare to stand strong, look up, and consider afresh what God's resurrection POWER can do in, through, and around you! Only those who've walked through the valley of the shadow will truly grasp the power of redemption on the other side. Jesus withholds NO good thing from those who walk intimately with Him. He's not the reason you suffer; He's with you in the storm. He is your Shelter, Deliverer, and Strong Tower. He's Your Redeemer, Savior, and Friend. He's your Prince of Peace and Sure Defender. Find your footing again. Engage your faith. Embrace a right perspective. Trust Jesus with your whole heart and see what love will do.

Let's Pray . . .

Precious Lord, You're so patient with me! Thank You for Your goodness, Your kindness, and Your grace. I'm so grateful that You're not finished with me yet! Help me again today, Lord, to grasp how wide and how deep, how strong and how true, how powerful and how perfect Your love is for me. Fill me afresh with a capacity to know You. Grant me a heart that sees You and a faith that trusts You. I declare that Your promises are true for me! I refuse to be bullied by my fears or paralyzed by the enemy's threats. I look away from him and up to You. You are the one I adore. You are the one my heart beats for. And You will lead me safely home. Right here, in the midst of this battle, Lord, show me how You've strengthened me here. Show me how to stand firm in this place. And put that fire in my soul so I can stand up and be counted as one who knows Your love and stands in my identity because of You. In Jesus' perfect name, I pray, Amen.

Praying God's Word

Write out a personalized prayer and weave in the truths of the following Scripture. Make the declaration that no matter what you're facing right now, nothing can separate you from the love of God!

> No, despite all these things, overwhelming victory is ours through Christ, who loved us.
>
> Romans 8:37 NLT

—————————————————————————————————

—————————————————————————————————

—————————————————————————————————

A POWERFUL WORD: *God Always Wins*

Battles are scary, and when I am in the middle of one, I'm often tempted to plot out a strategy or devise a clever Plan B in case God doesn't show up in time. But the more I get to know the Battle God of the Bible, the more I trust Him to deal ruthlessly with my enemies in His way and time. In the end, He will win. He always does.[5]

Personal Reflection

1. In what way is the enemy messing with you? How does he taunt you, threaten you, or bait you to take your eyes off of God?
2. What lies has he spewed that have felt true to you?
3. Since we know he's a liar, turn those lies around, spend a few prayerful moments with God and see if you can't discern what's actually true for you here.

4. What do you sense *is* God's truth for you in this place? Write it down.

5. Think about your current battle and what it takes for you to continually stand in faith. How is this battle making you a better warrior?

6. Spend a moment and pray for someone you know (or don't know) who may be struggling in the same way you do. Ask the Lord to encourage her today.

7. This one will push you out of your comfort zone, but you're ready for it: I dare you to get up on your feet and take your stand. Declare who you are, Whose you are, and that your God watches over you in battle. Say it out loud and put that enemy and his threats under your feet.

Group Reflection

1. In what area of life does the ground feel shaky beneath your feet? Where do you need courage and encouragement today?

2. Tell about a time when you felt cornered by fear or discouragement. How did you find your footing again?

3. What is God saying to you in this current season of life? What does obedience look like for you here?

4. Looking back over some of the battles you've faced, what would you say are your takeaways from those trials? Do you have a firmer grasp on God's promises? His character? Your identity? Explain.

5. What do you know to be true about God now that you didn't know before some of the battles you've faced? Encourage someone in your group today with what you know to be true about God.

6. Once you get through a particular battle and you find God faithful once again, do you find yourself empowered to go forward and trust God more fully? Or do you feel tempted to shrink back and self-protect? Explain.

7. Spend some time praying for a renewed perspective and a more fiery faith.

Jesus, Your King

The fear of the LORD is the beginning of wisdom,
and knowledge of the Holy One is understanding.

Proverbs 9:10

9

Dare to Ask

With Humility

Oh, how often we thwart God's interventions on our behalf by taking up our own cause or by striking a blow in our own defense! May God grant each of us this silent power and submissive spirit.

A.B. Simpson, as quoted in *Streams in the Desert*

Humble yourselves, therefore, under God's mighty hand, that he may lift you up in due time.

1 Peter 5:6

I've struggled with fear my whole life. But that hasn't kept me from reacting hastily in ways that could have gotten me into trouble. I guess I'm a fighter at heart. I'm easily frustrated by bullies and overwhelmed with compassion for the poor soul at the bottom of the pile. Perhaps because I've been that soul at the bottom of the pile.

Even so, when you consider how fear has been my constant companion, you'd think I'd know better than to run headlong into a battle God hasn't called me to, or to react out of my emotions when I should have instead responded to the still, small voice of God within me.

For example, once during my many months of bed rest due to high-risk pregnancies, I took a risk that dizzied me with fear *after* the fact.

On my way home from a doctor's appointment, I noticed a group of kids beating up a small boy. I slammed on my brakes. Honked my horn. Got out of my car. And then I marched my six-month pregnant belly right into the middle of that fight. I yanked one arm after another off of this young boy until he stood alone. I gave the bullies a piece of my mind and made sure the boy got home safely.

Immediately afterward I sat on my couch and rehearsed the scene in my mind. I rubbed my hardened belly. I drank lots of water. I found a focal point on the wall and took one deep breath after another, hoping I could stop the contractions and slow down my heart rate before Kev got home.

What was I thinking, risking my own baby's life like that? That's the point. I wasn't thinking about or even listening to what the Lord might have wanted to say to me. I *reacted* to my angst when I should have *responded* to the Lord's direction. I'm thinking He would have shown me how I could have helped that boy without taking such a risk.

Then there was the time when, while I was in the process of reacting foolishly, the Lord stopped me in my tracks. Thank You, Jesus. I remember that moment like it was yesterday.

I walked briskly through the mall, ready to head out the door, when suddenly I remembered I'd forgotten to pick up something from a particular store. I turned on a dime and smashed right into a guy who'd been following me too close. He was reaching for my purse when I smashed into him. He stared at me wide-eyed, then whipped around and sprinted away.

And I took off after him.

I zigzagged around shoppers, secretly impressed with my own athletic agility, when suddenly I heard the whisper in my heart, *"So what are you going to do with him once you catch him?"* Obviously I hadn't thought this all the way through. So I stopped running toward the enemy and decided instead to find the authorities and report the thug.

Submit to God

I covered this passage in the DVD companion that goes with my book *Your Beautiful Purpose*, but it's important to highlight here. Read this passage from James 4:7:

> Submit yourselves, then, to God. Resist the devil, and he will flee from you.

We want to prevail in spiritual battle. We want power in our prayers. We want to see results. And we have dreams and desires we long to see fulfilled. Yet at times our prayers seem to bounce off the ceiling, or go unanswered.

Sometimes God delays the breakthrough so He can prepare *us* to steward the gift or opportunity He's about to entrust to us. As I often say, *He makes us wait because He's making us ready.*

But other times *we're* the reason we've not seen a breakthrough. Sometimes we're our own hindrance to our answered prayers.

When answers seem slow to come, when the battle rages on, and when we wonder why the enemy continues to harass us like he does, we need to step back and take an inventory of our attitudes and actions. Our choices are often our biggest roadblocks to a thriving, powerful prayer life.

> Search me, O God, and know my heart; test me and
>   know my anxious thoughts.
> Point out anything in me that offends you, and lead me
>   along the path of everlasting life.
>   Psalm 139:23–24 NLT

And remember, prayer isn't just about getting what we want from God, although He really is a good Father and gives amazing gifts to His children. But prayer is ultimately about becoming who we were always meant to be in Christ. It's about an ongoing, intimate dialogue with the One who put the stars in their place. He is the King. He's returning as the King. He's placed us on the earth for a very distinct purpose. And our calling requires a listening ear and a humble heart. We can't do this kingdom life without clear and open communication with our heavenly Father or without a humble, teachable heart.

God makes us wait because He's making us ready.

Look again at the passage from James 4:7; the first word in this verse is *submit*. This is a military term in this context, and calls for us to *get back in rank*.

How do we get out of rank, exactly? Here are a few attitudes that stifle a prayerful process within you. May you pause and humbly work your way through this list:

- Hold a grudge
- Refuse to forgive
- Complain and grumble
- Usurp God-given authority
- Disobey

- Gossip
- Embrace selfish pride or selfish ambition
- Embrace envy and jealousy

There are more prayer deterrents than these, but suffice it to say, these are all gateway sins that open the door to the enemy's influence in our lives. We must remember that the enemy of our souls is a legalist and will look for any legal grounds by which to distract, derail, diminish, or discourage us from our life's calling. He sees our potential, he understands our authority (even better than we do), and he'll do whatever he can to knock us out of rank.

We are citizens of the Lord's army, and like it or not, we need to stay in rank and respect God's order of things. Let's look at a few passages to support this idea:

If I had cherished sin in my heart, the LORD would not have listened.

Psalm 66:18

Therefore, rid yourselves of all malice and all deceit, hypocrisy, envy, and slander of every kind.

1 Peter 2:1

You used to do these things when your life was still part of this world. But now is the time to get rid of anger, rage, malicious behavior, slander, and dirty language. . . . Make allowance for each other's faults, and forgive anyone who offends you. Remember, the Lord forgave you, so you must forgive others.

Colossians 3:7–8, 13 NLT

When you follow the desires of your sinful nature, the results are very clear: sexual immorality, impurity, lustful pleasures, idolatry, sorcery, hostility, quarreling, jealousy, outbursts of anger, selfish ambition, dissension, division, envy, drunkenness, wild parties, and other sins like these. Let me tell you again, as I have before, that anyone living that sort of life will not inherit the Kingdom of God.

Galatians 5:19–21 NLT

For jealousy and selfishness are not God's kind of wisdom. Such things are earthly, unspiritual, and demonic. For wherever there is jealousy and selfish ambition, there you will find disorder and evil of every kind.

James 3:15–16 NLT

The first step toward getting back in rank is to humble ourselves before the Lord. God loves a humble heart. He can't resist humility. And when we bow low and look up, when we surrender our hearts, our agendas, and our toxic attitudes, Jesus rises up on our behalf. First He helps us win the battle within, where battles are won and lost. Then He teaches us to stand in the authority He has given us.

A.W. Tozer offers this powerful insight:

Strange as it may seem, we often win over our enemies only after we have first been soundly defeated by the Lord Himself. God often conquers our enemies by conquering us . . . When God foresees that we must meet a deadly opponent, He assures our victory by bringing us down in humbleness at His own feet. After that, everything is easy. We have put ourselves in a position where God can fight for us, and in a situation like that, the outcome is decided from eternity.[1]

Scripture tells us the enemy prowls around, looking for a weak spot, any kind of opening in our lives so he can devour us. His goal isn't to poke fun at us or hurt our feelings. His goal is to destroy us. Spiritual warfare is no joke. And the enemy is not playing games. If we harbor sin and toxic attitudes in our hearts, the enemy of our souls will take our cue as his green light, and he'll leverage his opportunity to wreck our lives when the time is right.

So our first and most important step is to humble ourselves, recognize our own wayward ways, and acknowledge our need before our King.

When we surrender our hearts, our agendas, and our toxic attitudes, Jesus rises up on our behalf.

How do we repent? We acknowledge to Him that we've changed our mind about trying to handle things our own way, and we decide once again to follow Him on His terms and to seek Him with a pure heart.

> Dear friends, if our hearts do not condemn us, we have confidence before God and receive from him anything we ask, because we keep his commands and do what pleases him. And this is his command: to believe in the name of his Son, Jesus Christ, and to love one another as he commanded us. The one who keeps God's commands lives in him, and he in them. And this is how we know that he lives in us: We know it by the Spirit he gave us.
>
> 1 John 3:21–24

> God blesses those whose hearts are pure, for they will see God.
>
> Matthew 5:8

Here's an important point to remember: When we are guilty of sin, it does not diminish our heir status any more than disobedience diminishes an adopted child's identity as a family member. Have you adopted a child, or know someone who has? Do you see that child as less of a family member when they act like the humans they are?

Jesus knew who He was getting when He adopted us—when He grafted us into His family tree. Amazing, yes? To the extent we embrace that we are fully loved and profoundly accepted, we will live in the abundant life-freedom God intended for us all along. That said, the Father does discipline those He loves, and if we're out of rank, He'll let us know.

As loved sons and daughters, we live in the privilege of our heir status (regardless of how we behave), all because of Christ's profound victory on the cross. And yet as loved, obedient sons and daughters, God beckons us to walk in the purposes and power of our heir status.

What does it mean to embrace our heir purpose? We believe and embrace the following:

We've been bought with a price and are called to live worthy of His name.

We've been blessed to be a blessing.

We've been made rich in the things of God, that many might come to know Him through us.

We're promised access to God's presence, power, and promises to see His purposes fulfilled on the earth.

We've been given an unshakable identity in Christ so we can love people well, regardless of their opinions of us.

We walk in our heir purpose when we use our spiritual wealth, privilege, and status for the greater good of the kingdom. It's the difference between a foolish heir who squanders his inheritance (and will one day answer for it), and the wise heir who takes what his father has entrusted to him and makes something if it. Some of Christ's royal heirs will squander their influence because they don't see the value of what God has entrusted to them. Are they still heirs? Absolutely. Are they still loved? For sure. Have they pleased God with their lives? Not so much. Scripture is clear that one day we will give an account for how we stewarded all God entrusted to us. We have a royal responsibility to represent the King and His kingdom well. Not for love but because of it.

Here's the exciting part. James 4:7 tells us that once we submit to God and get things right with Him, *then* we can stand and resist that enemy of our souls. We take our rightful place, we raise our shield of faith, and we tell the enemy to get lost and leave us alone. And how does he respond? He flees from us. He runs for his life. He changes his plans and tries to get away from us.

To stay powerful in prayer, we must stay in step with Jesus. True, we are saved and established by grace. We have no hope apart from God's great love and Christ's victory on the cross. Furthermore, God's grace empowers us to obey God. And that matters because we—as God's children—are called to obey Him and walk in His ways. Read Andrew Murray's beautiful words:

> The first lesson taught here is our need for a disposition of forgiveness. The Scripture admonishes us to forgive one another as God, for Christ's sake, has forgiven us. God's full and free forgiveness is the standard for our forgiveness. If we are reluctant or halfhearted about it, which is not forgiveness at all, neither will God forgive us. *Every prayer depends upon our faith in God's pardoning grace.* If God dealt with us according to our sins, not one prayer would be heard. Pardon opens the door to all of God's love and blessing: *because God has pardoned our sins, our prayers can prevail.* The ground for answered prayer is God's forgiving love. *When God's love and forgiveness have taken possession of our hearts, we will pray in faith and we will live in love.*[2]

So Ask!

Now that we've established that the tone of our lives impacts the power in our prayers, we can move on to the fun part. As we walk in step with the Holy Spirit, God's desires become our desires—His tastes, our tastes. We become conduits to His heart and passion for the world. The things we desire to see in our lives and the lives of our loved ones are so often the very things He desires for us.

Scripture tells us a number of things about prevailing prayer:

- When we pray in accordance to God's will, we can be assured that God will answer (1 John 5:14–15).
- If/when we abide in Christ and thrive in Him, we can ask God for what's on our hearts and He will answer (John 15:7).
- Faith pleases the heart of God, and as we passionately pursue Him, He rewards us (Hebrews 11:6).
- Since it's the Father's will that we bear much fruit, He has promised to answer our prayers for an abundant, fruitful life (John 15:16).
- We can cast our cares upon the Lord, and He promises to sustain us (Psalm 55:22).
- As we delight in the Lord, He establishes us and grants us our heart's desires (Psalm 37:4).
- The persistent prayer of the righteous person accomplishes great and powerful things (James 5:16).
- God invites us out of fearful anxiety and into a place of thankful, hopeful, peaceful expectancy (Philippians 4:6–8).

What's on Your Heart?

Whatever's on your heart today, know this: The Father cares deeply for you. He delights in every detail of your life. He's moved by your faith. He hears you when you call on Him. And His promises are true. We have unshakable ground to stand on in Christ. And when we believe Him for who He is and do what He says, then we can know that His power and His promises will impact our story. The enemy runs scared and we become powerful, prayerful saints.

So what about those dreams in your heart? Have you persisted in prayer? Or has it been more of a hit-and-miss proposition for you? We'll talk more about passionate persistence in chapter 10, so be encouraged.

But today, open up your hands and ask the Lord to invade your life, to settle your heart, to inspire your dreams, and to carry your burdens. Ask Him to multiply your offering, to open closed doors, to move in the hearts and minds of your loved ones, to foil the plans of the wicked, to establish the plans of the righteous, and to make a way where there's been no way.

Thank Him for all He's already accomplished in your life. And don't forget to listen for what He has to say to you. He wants to impart fresh wisdom to your soul. He has a fresh perspective for you to consider. And He wants to infuse fresh strength for the journey.

Think of it this way: We spend time going to the bank to withdraw money for our care. We spend time in the kitchen taking food out of the cupboards for our consumption. We spend time with friends for our company. And all these things are necessities in life. But more than these, we have Jesus. And what we possess in the richness of Christ and in all of the heavenly resources He has made available to us is far superior to any earthly resource we can see, taste, or touch.

So may we take God up on His promise to pour out His Spirit on us. May we take Him at His word and take His promises as they stand. May we take time in His presence that we might better understand His power and authority. There are riches in the heavenlies that are *ours for the taking*, because we've been made heirs of God.

Praise be to the God and Father of our Lord Jesus Christ, who has blessed us in the heavenly realms with every spiritual blessing in Christ.

Ephesians 1:3

May we stretch out our hands, stand on our tiptoes, and pray. Let's pray big, audacious, impossible prayers. And may we continue to listen, to learn, and to obey. *Anything* is possible with God.

Bold prayers honor God, and God honors bold prayers. God isn't offended by your biggest dreams or boldest prayers. He is offended by anything less. If your prayers aren't impossible to you, they are insulting to God. Why? Because they don't require divine intervention. But ask God to part the Red Sea, or make the sun stand still or float an iron axhead, and God is moved to omnipotent action. There is nothing God loves more than keeping promises, answering prayers, performing miracles, and fulfilling dreams. That is who He is. That is what He does.[3]

A Blessing for You

May you—above all else—see yourself as someone Jesus loves. May His affection for you heal you in the deepest ways and inspire you like nothing else ever has. May His saving grace and enabling power compel you to dream with Him, believe in Him, and take crazy faith-steps because of Him. May every lesser voice and every lying circumstance fall by the wayside so that all you hear is His voice in your ear, saying, "This is the way, walk in it." Nobody's opinion matters as much as God's. Nobody can save, heal, redeem, and refresh like Jesus. Walk intimately with Him today. His will for you is your best-case scenario.

Let's Pray . . .

Precious Lord, You are all I need. I humble myself before You and I invite You to have Your way in my life, in my story, in my hurts, hopes, and dreams. I give You full access to my soul and my character. I ask You to guide and provide, correct and redirect; show me what to say and what to pray, how to give and how to live. I know that You are a good Father, and that when You call me up, You're about to call me out, and I want to be ready. I see now that to the extent that I take seriously the call on my life, will You take seriously the prayers that come from my mouth. So I stand in faith, saved by grace, equipped by Your promises, and empowered by Your Spirit, and I pray boldly, audaciously, and expectantly. Do wonders in and through me, Lord. Give me eyes to see, ears to hear, and a heart to do Your will. In Your powerful, matchless name, I pray, Amen.

Praying God's Word

Write out a personalized prayer and weave in the truths of the following Scripture. Make the declaration that no matter what you're facing right now, nothing can separate you from the love of God!

Humble yourselves, therefore, under God's mighty hand,
that he may lift you up in due time.

1 Peter 5:6

_____

_____

_____

_____

A POWERFUL WORD: *Persevere in Prayer*

The great danger in this school of delayed answers is the temptation to think that it may not be God's will to give us what we ask. *But if our prayer is according to God's Word and under the leading of the Spirit, we must not give in to such fear.* Learn to give God time: time in your daily fellowship with Him, time to exercise the influence of His presence; time to prove its reality. He will lead us from faith to vision; we *shall* see the glory of God.[4]

Personal Reflection

1. Take a prayerful inventory of your soul today. If you find even a bit of unrest there, answer this question: What is God saying to you about the angst in your soul, or the fears in your heart?

2. Oftentimes we let go of the very things that breathe fresh life into our souls. Take a moment to ponder if you've let go of any of your life-giving disciplines. Make a plan today to shore up your days once again.

3. We also lose our passion for prayer when we squander our moments on things that do nothing but eat up our time. Consider doing a temporary fast on your indulgences if they've gotten the best of you lately.

4. Remember to *refuse* condemnation. This is always about invitation. And humility is always the first step. Where you've been striving, straining, or barely surviving, decide instead to humble yourself before the Lord today. Ask Him to infuse your heart with His provision and power.

5. Spend some time prayerfully forgiving those with whom you have the slightest grudge or feel even slightly offended by. Forgive yourself too. Pray blessings on them and on yourself.

6. Write out a list of six or seven impossible or audacious prayers—things you long to see God fulfill—ways you long

to see Him move. Tuck the list in your Bible and tackle those prayers every single day. Be sure to journal changes of heart or changes of circumstance.

7. Ask God for a fresh vision for your prayer life. Ask Him for promises from Scripture to attach to your prayer list. Keep your heart open to the idea that He will answer in His time and His way. That said, don't—for a moment—lose your sense of expectancy.

Group Reflection

1. Talk about a time you prayed earnestly for something but failed to receive the answer (or the answer was hugely delayed). How did that experience impact you?

2. Share about a time when you received a powerful, beyond-expected answer to your prayers.

3. Why do you suppose our heart attitude is so connected to the power of our prayers?

4. What spiritual disciplines are most life-giving to you (prayer, worship, fasting, journaling, serving, etc.)?

5. Oftentimes our tendency toward indulgence, excess, or disengagement baits us away from the spiritual disciplines that are so good for our souls. If you're willing, talk about where you are at when it comes to your time, your disciplines, and your prayer life. Ask for prayer if you need it. We all—in one way or another—tend to weave and wander and find our way back to that life-giving path again. Isn't it amazing how gracious and patient and kind God is? He loves us through every season of our lives.

6. If you're willing, share an audacious, impossible prayer request, something you long to see fulfilled.

7. What is God saying to you regarding this impossible dream? Are there any adjustments you sense He wants you to make?

10

Dare to Seek

With Passion

Think of the most challenging prayer requests in your life—a health issue, a financial issue, salvation for a wayward loved one, etc. Rather than sheepishly muttering a few half-hopeful, half doubting prayers about that issue, begin praying bold, audacious prayers and watch what God does.

Eric and Leslie Ludy, *Wrestling Prayer*

Always be joyful. *Never stop praying.* Be thankful in all circumstances, for this is God's will for you who belong to Christ Jesus.

1 Thessalonians 5:16–18 NLT

My husband used to be a workaholic. He's a great man. A godly man. But a man who, back then, couldn't help but trust himself to care for our family more than he trusted God to care for our family. We argued, we reasoned, we prayed. We did what we could to make the best of a situation that from my perspective just was not God's best for us.

At some point during our journey, I'd had enough. I felt beyond frustrated with my husband's bent toward striving, and with how his work atmosphere at the time seemed to drain him dry, which in turn impacted our home life.

I took up my case before God with such resolve, I would not be denied. It's like I grabbed the horns of the altar and refused to let go. I couldn't help myself. If God didn't come through for us, I feared that our family life would fall *far* short of what God had promised us.

Out on a limb I went. Facedown on the floor. I implored my God to move in my husband's heart and in his work situation. Each day I'd search Scripture for promises to anchor me, I'd cry out to the Holy Spirit for His presence to empower me, and I'd appeal to heaven for God to direct me. The more I prayed, the feistier I felt.

I knew God had more for Kevin, and more for us as a family. I knew my prayers lined up with God's will. And Scripture tells us that when we pray God's will, we can *be sure* that He not only hears us, but that *we will have* that for which we've asked Him.

> This is the confidence we have in approaching God: that if we ask anything according to his will, he hears us. And if we know that he hears us—whatever we ask—we know that we have what we asked of him.
>
> 1 John 5:14–15

Expectation vs. Expectancy

My mentor once told me, "Susie, it's important that you understand the difference between expectation and expectancy." She went on to say that expectation is actually premeditated disappointment. In other words, when we create our own perfect scenario, and expect God (or others) to come through for us in exactly the way we want them to, we set ourselves up for disappointment. This puts undue pressure on the relationship in a way that's unfair and unsustainable.

When we dictate our expectations to God and then we're surprised when He doesn't jump through our hoops, we eventually lose heart. We find ourselves weakened in faith, and we reason that maybe it doesn't really pay to pray, after all.

I think of it this way: When we develop an expectation, it's like we hold up a finger-sized picture frame and expect God (or someone) to paint a picture to our liking, exactly like the one we've pictured in our head.

I'm sure you've had plenty of vacations, holidays, date nights, and special outings that have turned out nothing like you'd envisioned, right? And what do we do as a result? We resolve to let go of any expectation. We lower the bar. We leave it all open to happenstance.

Now, a part of this idea of letting go of our expectations is a sign of maturity. But another part of this mind-set reveals a lack of expectancy that something divine just might happen. We call ourselves believers, but are we *really*?

Do we truly believe . . .

- God is at work on the earth today.
- He hears us when we pray.
- He's the same yesterday, today, and forever.
- He keeps His promises.
- He's not a respecter of people but of faith.
- He draws near to those who humbly worship Him.
- Nothing is too difficult for Him.
- It's *impossible* for Him to fail us.

Do we really believe what God says about Himself?

To live with expectancy is to live with an ear bent toward heaven. It's to repeatedly look above our circumstances, knowing that God *is* involved in our everyday lives. To live with expectancy is to pray with passion and conviction, to cultivate humble contentment in our current circumstances while at the same time *tenaciously believing* that our prayers matter. The expectant heart passionately believes that any day now, God just might break through.

To live with expectancy is to throw away our puny picture frame and give God time and space to work out His plans for us with the understanding that there's always a mystery to following God. He's a miracle-working God, and He often breaks through in ways we couldn't have imagined and at a time when we least expect Him to.

It's not that we expect too much from God. In fact, we often expect too little. Our idea of what breakthrough looks like frequently falls short of what God has in mind for us. His breakthroughs always bear fruit, always bless others (not just us), and always accomplish His purposes on the earth.

Sometimes God waits longer than we'd like to break through, so that He can accomplish more than we ever imagined.

As much as we want Him to tidy up our smaller story, He refuses to stay stuck there. Or to let us stay stuck there. Sometimes He waits longer than we'd like to break through, so that He can accomplish more than we ever imagined.

Fruit-Bearing Breakthroughs

The more I prayed about my husband's work situation, the stronger I felt in my soul. I just knew I was on track and praying for something that God Himself wanted for us as a family. And the more I prayed, the more I understood that the outcome, the answer, could unfold in any number of ways.

Maybe we'd take a pay cut and have to figure out how to make it on a lesser income. Or maybe we'd have to move away from family and friends. Maybe we'd have to go through a difficult time to be reminded once again what matters most in life.

I've written about this in other books, so I'll only briefly mention it here, but suffice it to say, right in the midst of my prayer pursuit, my husband was diagnosed with cancer.

I don't believe for a moment that God gave Kevin cancer to teach him a lesson, but I do believe that God allowed something the enemy meant for evil, and He turned it for good in our lives. Kevin had exhausted himself at that company, yet his employer continually kept the carrot-reward just out of his reach.

Kevin often says that God loved him enough to allow him to lie down in his own weakness so he could look up to Jesus and find a new strength in Him. And that's exactly what happened.

And there *was* a company in town that Kev had his eye on. They managed large-scale construction projects (his forte) and they treated their employees well. So while I repeatedly put my expectations on the table before God, I also purposefully zeroed in on that company and asked God, if it were His will, that He'd open a door for Kev to work there.

One morning over coffee I told Kev about the focus of my prayers. I hugged my mug and confessed, "I'm praying God opens a door at that company for you. You're great at managing those big jobs and it just seems like a great fit for you."

My husband wanted to let me down gently so he carefully said, "Well, honey, that's so kind of you to pray such a prayer, but you've got to know that *nobody* ever leaves that company. They only retire from there. The owners give about half of their profits back to their people. They treat their employees really well. And nobody's up for retirement quite yet. But thanks for thinking of me."

Did I mention I'm a bit feisty? I couldn't help myself. I just replied, "Well, watch my dust." He chuckled.

Meanwhile, I dug in and prayed like I never have prayed before. I prayed in the morning. I prayed in the evening. I prayed when I folded clothes and when I prepared the kids' lunch. I prayed when I exercised. I alternately prayed for an open door at this company, and for God to move my heart toward His best will for us in case this particular desire of my heart was outside of His plans for us.

As with *any* prayer pursuit, God used this process to address my own areas of soul unrest and fear. I needed to learn afresh that my hope wasn't in Kevin. My hope was in God. And my joy wasn't contingent upon Kevin getting a new job or in me finally getting my way. My true sustainable joy came from Christ, which I learned was contingent on the strength and perspective *I* chose to embrace right in the midst of my unanswered prayer.

This process wasn't just about getting Kevin out of a life-draining job. It was also about getting the fear and angst and disappointment out of me. God's process both healed and strengthened me, and prepared Kev for his next place of promise.

One day Kev came home from work and looked stunned— awestruck, even. I glanced up from my pile of laundry and asked, "You okay?"

He replied, "Are you still praying that I'll get a job with that company?"

I smiled. "Why? Did they call?"

He scratched the back of his neck, nodded his head, and said, "Um, yes. The owner actually called and took me to lunch today. Apparently a couple of their men retired early. He wants me to come and work for them. He made me a very generous offer."

We could not have fathomed how God intended to use this breakthrough to change our lives. Kevin flourished in his new company. He grew as a project manager. Grew even more as a godly father and a husband. He became more kingdom-minded than he ever was before. In fact, the answer to that prayer continues to bear fruit today.

Kev works hard at his construction management job during the week, and he works his tail off when we have an occasional retreat or a conference over the weekend. He's actually managing more now than he did during those workaholic years, but he manages the "much" God has entrusted to him with grace, margin, and plenty of time for rest. I honestly marvel at the thought of it.

When Kev is on the job site, his guys love to banter with him. They tell Kev that they're going hunting or fishing over the weekend. Then they ask, "So what are *you* doing this weekend, Kev?" He narrows his eyes and smiles and says, "You already know what I'm doing. I'm going to another women's retreat."

Ha ha. Now that's a *real* man, wouldn't you say?

Burdens and Bridges

When we lose our sense of expectancy, we too easily acclimate to a low level of misery during our time on this earth. While it's true that in this world, we will have trials and tribulations (Jesus said as much), it's also true that He came to destroy the works of the devil (1 John 3:8), to save us (John 3:16–17), to free us (Galatians 5:1), and to give us an abundant life (John 10:10).

Sometimes we put up with too much from that enemy of our souls when we have the authority to break free from the snares and the traps that he constantly sets for us. I love A.W. Tozer's sentiments here:

Brethren, God never meant for us to be kicked around like a football. He wants us to be humble and let Him do the chastening when necessary. But when the devil starts tampering with you, dare to resist Him! I stand for believing in God and defying the devil—and our God loves that kind of courage among His people. If you are still wrapped in grave clothes and great fears lie upon you, it is time for you to dare to rise and in sweet faith in the risen Jesus Christ declare: "I will not take this any longer. I am a child of God—why should I go mourning all the day?" Will God answer? "All right, My child." He will answer as the burden rolls away, "I have waited long to hear you say that. Jesus is the Victor and in Him you overcome!"[1]

Recently our friend Pastor Nate Ruch offered this great insight during one of his sermons: Hidden in our struggles are previews to a future vision that we don't quite yet see. We need to keep a file during such times. Our burdens often become a bridge to our future.

What's bothering you today? Is there something in your life that you've put up with that God wants to deliver you from? Have you lost expectancy after too many dashed expectations?

Maybe it's time to up your game and seek God earnestly regarding your life, your future, and His promises. If you seek Him, you will find Him. He rewards those who earnestly seek after Him.

How might He reward you in your pursuit? I dare you to get a vision for your next place of promise. I challenge you to open your hands and give God access to the angst in your soul. And I pray you'll more quickly discern the difference between surrendering to your circumstances, and surrendering to God in your circumstances.

Time and time again for us, our burdens have proven to be a bridge to our future. I tend not to fear obstacles like I used to. And I'm quicker now to realize that when needs arise they're just opportunities to remember afresh that God is a good Father who promises to care for His children. I'm learning to cultivate a lifestyle of fierce faith and humble expectancy. The God who sees everything is always on the move. He searches for sincere faith in the hearts of His followers who are on the earth *today*.

I have a whole new appreciation for the necessity of earnestly seeking God and His will for our lives. First we seek His will. Then we pray His promises. God *invites* us to prevail in prayer, to wait patiently, and to fully entrust the outcomes to Him.

I pray you'll more quickly discern the difference between surrendering to your circumstances, and surrendering to God in your circumstances.

> Patient endurance is what you need now, so that you will continue to do God's will. Then you will receive all that he has promised.
>
> Hebrews 10:36 NLT

While I'm very careful not to preach a message that conveys God as a means to an end—because HE IS the beginning and the end—neither do I want to swing to the other extreme and preach a worm-theology that glorifies our hardships and denies God's promises. God is always good. His promises are always true. And one way or another, He will always make a way for us.

> Being anchored in the goodness of God isn't always going to be a rational thing. It's a stubborn, unrelenting determination not to let the hardships of life downsize the bigness of God.[2]

If we adjust our theology to always match our experiences, we'll miss the wonder and the power and the majesty of God's involvement in our lives. Faith won't always feel like a rational choice, but know this: His promises always call us upward. His power always compels us onward. And His presence always reminds us that He Himself is the greatest gift of all. And we already *have* Him. So we're blessed profoundly. Right here. Right now. Let's pray like we have a God in heaven who hears us when we pray and who moves on our faith. Because we do. And He does.

A Blessing for You

May God Himself pour out His Spirit on you and every member of your family! May you all know and experience God's love more deeply and profoundly than you ever have before. May He heal you in mind, body, and spirit! May He awaken your faith, engage your heart, and empower your prayers! May you begin to see what He wants you to see, say what He wants you to say, and pray what He wants you to pray. You belong to Him! You are His ambassadors on the earth today. He is good. His promises are true, and He will make a way for you. May you lift your hands in praise for all He's done and all He's about to do. He is always good and you are always loved. Thank You, Jesus, Amen.

Let's Pray . . .

Precious Lord, I surrender to Your will. I humble myself before You, open my hands, and ask, speak to my heart, dear Lord. Show me where I've lost expectancy. Teach me how to hope in You alone. Deal with those places in my heart where I've settled, let go, and quit fighting. I want to be a warrior for You! Help me to take Your promises as they stand. Teach me to walk with wisdom and discernment. I'm an heir. Teach me to live like one, pray like one, and believe like one. Your victory on the cross made all the difference. Help me to live like that's true. Give me the holy gumption to go after the things You've promised

*me. Overwhelm me with a fresh sense of Your goodness,
Your grace, and Your power. In Jesus' name, I pray, Amen.*

Praying God's Word

Write out a personalized prayer and weave in the truths of the following Scripture. Make the declaration that in Christ Jesus, God has given you authority over the power of the enemy!

We demolish arguments and every pretension that sets itself up against the knowledge of God, and we take captive every thought to make it obedient to Christ.

2 Corinthians 10:5

_____

_____

_____

A POWERFUL WORD: *You Are His*

Remember who you are; you are God's child. You've been bought by the most precious commodity in the history of the universe: the blood of Christ. You are indwelled by the Spirit of the living God. You are being equipped for an eternal assignment that will empower you to live in the very presence of God. You have been set apart for a holy calling. You are his.[3]

Personal Reflection

1. What past disappointment still impacts your prayer life today?
2. Spend a moment with your Bible and your journal. *Seek* God in this place regarding that particular disappointment.

Remember, if you seek Him, He will be found by you. He wants you to be free more than you want to be free. Ask Him for a fresh perspective. Ask Him to show you a truth that sets you free.

3. In what area of life have you settled for mediocrity or even a low level of misery because you've been afraid of further disappointment?

4. Start small, if you have to, but ask God to breathe fresh life into your heart; ask Him for a fresh vision for what He might want to do in this situation. Search the Scripture for a promise to hang on to.

5. Dare to pause and ask God to search your heart; ask Him to show you where you're offended, unbelieving, or full of angst. If you're ready, confess your need before Him and ask Him to do a *new* thing in you. He loves you. He invites you to something more. May you trust Him enough to break free and follow Him more earnestly.

6. What's the difference between surrendering *to* your circumstances and surrendering *to God in* your circumstances?

7. Think about both options (surrendering to your circumstances and surrendering to God in your circumstances). How might this very important choice impact your story?

Group Reflection

1. Share about a time when you prayed earnestly for something and it didn't turn out the way you'd hoped. How did that experience impact your prayer life and even your relationship with God?

2. Dare to ask the group for their thoughts on your experience (and dare to share your insights about their experiences).

3. In what area of life have you lost your sense of expectancy and hope? If you dare, ask your friends for some encouragement and perspective. Be open to wisdom they may have for you.

4. Share about a time you persisted in prayer, and God broke through in a way that was beyond what you'd hoped for.

5. Share your thoughts on the difference between surrendering to your circumstances and surrendering to God in your circumstances.

6. Talk about how this one very important choice (surrendering to your circumstances or surrendering to God in your circumstances) can impact a person's story.

7. What are you believing God for right now? Is there anything on your prayer list that seems impossible unless God breaks through? Explain.

11

Dare to Knock

With Confidence

Your sin has not disqualified you from seeking His help in the heat of battle. When you feel surrounded by accusers with rocks in hand, you can be certain that God is not one of them. Our good, compassionate God lavishes mercy instead of anger on all who ask. Isn't that the best news ever?

Bo Stern, *The God Who Fights For You*

"Keep on asking, and you will receive what you ask for. Keep on seeking, and you will find. Keep on knocking, and the door will be opened to you. For everyone who asks, receives. Everyone who seeks, finds. And to everyone who knocks, the door will be opened."

Matthew 7:7–8 NLT

The other day, my son Jake called and asked me a question that was an unusual one for him. I hopped off the treadmill, sat down on the edge, and leaned in to listen to what pressed on his heart that day. "Mom, um, you know how I got my road bike back from Luke recently so I could sell it to buy drums? Well, I took it out for a ride today and I had an experience with God unlike I've had in a very long time. I felt a strong sense of God's presence and even His joy. I know this sounds crazy, but it made me second-guess if I should sell this bike, you know? You and Dad bought it for me at a significant turning point in my life. I love it for so many reasons. But I'm feeling called to get back into drumming, especially on a worship team, and it's not financially responsible to hang on to this bike *and* buy the drums even if I can afford it, *is* it?"

This from a son who refused any financial help when he first graduated from college and moved to Nashville where he lived on a ten-dollar-per-hour job and the garden he planted in the back-yard of the rental house in which he lived. We knew he struggled financially, but the few times we offered help, he replied, "No, I've got this. I want to do this." We respected him greatly for his conviction and tenacity.

Jake continued, "I'll need the drums when I eventually play on a worship team, whereas the bike is just for my pleasure. I'd feel guilty having both. But there's something about this bike that's so tied to my heart and my history. I normally don't ask questions like this. I'd just do what I had to do. But for some reason, I felt I needed to run this one by you and hear your thoughts."

I said, "Son, I love that you're wrestling with this question, especially given the materialistic, entitlement society that we're immersed in. But in this particular case, I wonder. Might God want you to have *both* the bike and the drums? And are the drums a more spiritual possession than the bike? I mean, for me, when I exercise, I so sense God's presence and His good-ness to me. The longer I walk with Christ, the less I tend to compartmentalize my spiritual life, you know? He's with me in all things, and *every* good gift comes from His hand."

Jake and I went back and forth and processed why this notion seemed so difficult for him to swallow. Something about it tied him up. He couldn't bring himself to accept that such an extravagant gift might actually be God's idea, not his. So I asked one probing question after another and reflected on certain memories that had shaped his thinking over the years.

We revisited an experience from his teenage years. Though he was a really compliant kid, one particular day, he took the bait from his prodding friends and used my Chevy Blazer to do doughnuts in a parking lot freshly covered with snow.

Long story short, he pulled into a parking lot, spun around, and hit a concrete structure, which caused about three thousand dollars' worth of damage to my truck.

We sat down as a family and processed what had happened. Jake's little brothers asked him questions and he humbly answered them. Every single one. Kevin looked at Jake with that fatherly strength and said something to this effect: "Son, you've just taken a huge withdrawal from the 'trust' account. And we have to deal with the consequences of this costly choice. *However*, I want you to know something: Your trust account is *not* empty. We love you. We still trust you and totally respect you. You *are* a trust-worthy son."

I sat on the edge of my treadmill and held the phone close to my ear. "Jake, do you remember what you were doing when Dad said those words to you?"

He whispered, "Um, no. I don't."

I continued, "You gripped the arms of the chair and looked down at your feet. You couldn't even look up at him."

Jake went silent on the other end.

"Honey? Are you there?"

His voice cracked, and he whispered, "Mom, I always knew you and Dad handled that incident brilliantly, but I couldn't exactly remember how it all played out that day. Something got in me when I made a choice that so defied the things I care most about. I loved and respected both you and Dad so much. I could never imagine that I'd do what I did. My own choice cut me deep and I've never really been able to get past it. In fact, I had no idea that my posture was so shut down when Dad spoke to me. I faintly remember his words now, but they sure didn't go in back then."

"That's shame, son. *That's* what got in you that day. It's shame. And though you're a man of integrity and have never wanted our financial help in your young adult years, I wonder if mixed in with that nobility of yours is a stronghold of shame that won't allow you to receive help. Could it be that underneath your strong work ethic is a heart that doesn't believe that your parents (or your heavenly Father, for that matter) might want to lavish a goodness on you that goes beyond your efforts or even beyond what you think you deserve?" My voice cracked as I asked such probing questions.

Again, more silence from Jake.

Then, my big, husky, first-born son started to cry. I sucked in a sob. "Oh, honey. Can I just tell you? I love you so much. And that shame? It's *not* from God and it's not from us."

We both struggled to find our words. He then asked me, "Is *this* what has held me back all these years? Is this why it's difficult for me to receive out-of-the-ordinary kinds of gifts? And why I don't ask for your help or for God's? Because of shame?"

As I thought back to Jake's wanderings through his college and young adult years, I couldn't help but wonder if shame had a self-perpetuating nature—one that repeatedly seduces, then accuses, finds you weak and wandering, only to seduce and accuse again until you're caught in a cycle that pulls you farther from grace, not toward it.

Was it shame that baited Jake away from the Father's heart and kept him away for the past several years? Jake waited for me to answer his question, *Is this what has held me back all of these years?*

"I think so, honey." I'd have given anything to hug him at that moment. "But imagine how delightful your relationship with God could be if you could learn to approach Him and even pursue Him with assurance and confidence because you're *convinced* that He is good and that He has set His affections upon *you*. I'd say, right now, you're missing the best parts of this relationship. But what joy for you to discover an unhindered, joy-filled relationship with your Father who loves you and loves to lavish His goodness upon you! Doing so will affect *every* aspect of your life: your work, your play, your bike riding, and your morning coffee with your wife. Joy and confidence are accessible even amidst the battles you face. Not just in those moments when you're doing something 'spiritual' like drumming on a worship team."

> Did you notice that in addition to forgiveness of sin, healing and redemption, and the experience of love and compassion, God satisfies our desires with good things?[1]

Sometimes we can easily spot His gifts and His grace; other times, not so much. But how often does shame keep us from audaciously running into the arms of our Father not only to receive grace just after we've blown it, but to dare to ask for things we could never earn, deserve, or acquire on our own?

After my conversation with Jake, I wondered if shame was just a negative emotion and a skewed mind-set. Or is it an actual parasitic force that drains life, takes life, and keeps us from the life God has always intended for us? So I asked God to teach me more about shame. A couple days later a friend handed me a book, out of the blue. Its title? *The Soul of Shame.* Read on:

> Shame is not just a consequence of something our first parents did in the Garden of Eden. It is the emotional weapon that evil

uses to (1) corrupt our relationships with God and each other, and (2) disintegrate any and all gifts of vocational vision and creativity. These gifts include any area of endeavor that promotes goodness, beauty and joy in and for the lives of others, whether that be teaching our first graders, loving our spouse well, managing forests, conducting healing prayer services, creating a new medical technology, offering psychotherapy or composing symphonies. *Shame is a primary means to prevent us from using the gifts we have been given. And those gifts enable us to flourish as a light-bearing community of Jesus followers.* . . . Shame, therefore, is not simply an unfortunate, random, emotional event that came with us out of the primordial evolutionary soup. *It is both a source and result of evil's active assault on God's creation, and a way for evil to try to hold out until the new heaven and earth appear at the consummation of history.*[2]

If shame keeps us from the best of what God has for us, shouldn't we be more earnest in calling it what it is so we can shun the shame of our youth and thus *become* who God always intended us to be and *receive* all He has promised us? Consider what's true about some of the mind-sets we often embrace without even thinking about it:

- It's not humility that compels us to shy away from God and ask little from Him: it's shame.
- It's not integrity that keeps us from asking for God's help when we need it: it's pride, independence, and shame.
- It's not noble to go without something that God has promised to provide: it's an orphan mentality rooted in shame.
- It is not justice that keeps us far from God after we've blown it: it's shame.
- It's not kindness that keeps us from "bothering" God with our persistent requests: it's either spiritual laziness or shame.

How often does shame keep us from the kind of audacity in prayer and pursuit of fellowship that Jesus invites us to? Let's take a look at a parable of a woman who appeared to be shameless. In this context, she was a woman (not recognized in the court of law), she was poor (had no means to pay), and she had no one to advocate for her. Notice too that Jesus doesn't tell us this story to make the point that He'll finally answer us if we "bother" Him enough.

We don't have to try to convince Him to be good to us. In fact, He's the one trying to convince us to receive and walk in His goodness.

This parable is a lesson in contrasts. We don't have to try to convince Him to be good to us. In fact, *He's* the one trying to convince *us* to receive and walk in His goodness.

Now, let's look at the parable from Luke 18:1–8 (NLT):

One day Jesus told his disciples a story to show that they should always pray and never give up. "There was a judge in a certain city," he said, "who neither feared God nor cared about people. A widow of that city came to him repeatedly, saying, 'Give me justice in this dispute with my enemy.' The judge ignored her for a while, but finally he said to himself, 'I don't fear God or care about people, but this woman is driving me crazy. I'm going to see that she gets justice, because she is wearing me out with her constant requests!'" Then the Lord said, "Learn a lesson from this unjust judge. Even he rendered a just decision in the end. So don't you think God will surely give justice to his chosen people who cry out to him day and night? Will he keep putting them off? I tell you, he will grant justice to them quickly! But when the Son of Man returns, how many will he find on the earth who have faith?"

Here's what's true for the person who is in Christ, and is therefore His joint heir:

- We are recognized in the heavenly court and have every right to appear before the King; furthermore, we can be assured of His glad welcome (Ephesians 3:12; Hebrews 4:16).

- While we don't need financial means to cover our defense, we do need spiritual resources, and we have them in Christ Jesus. We're righteous. We're equipped. We're covered (Ephesians 1:3; 2 Corinthians 5:21).

- We have an advocate—Jesus Himself. He intercedes for us day and night. We're not bending the ear of an unrighteous judge in an effort to get his attention (1 John 2:1; Hebrews 7:25).

- We have the heart and the ear of our God who longs for us, loves us, and intends to finish what He started in us (Psalm 18:6; Philippians 1:6).

Prayer? Faith?

Jesus' parable opens with His reason for sharing it: *That we should pray and never give up.* Then He closes His story with a question: *But when the Son of Man returns, how many will He find on the earth who have faith?*

If Jesus invites us to pray and never give up, why are we not more audacious in our asking, believing, and receiving? If He's looking for faith on the earth, why does He—more often than not—find fear, anxiety, and worry in us, instead of faith? Why do we allow shame to pull us away when grace beckons us close?

We can persist in prayer when we remember our right standing before God (because of Christ's victory on the cross). We can be shameless when we remember we're blameless (because Christ's perfect and right standing have been imparted to us).

Let's look at a few more passages that speak to persistence in prayer:

Look to the LORD and his strength; seek his face always.

1 Chronicles 16:11

Be joyful in hope, patient in affliction, faithful in prayer.

Romans 12:12

Rejoice always, pray continually, give thanks in all circumstances; for this is God's will for you in Christ Jesus.

1 Thessalonians 5:16–18

Do not be anxious about anything, but in every situation, by prayer and petition, with thanksgiving, present your requests to God. And the peace of God, which transcends all understanding, will guard your hearts and your minds in Christ Jesus.

Philippians 4:6–7

Devote yourselves to prayer, being watchful and thankful.

Colossians 4:2

I used to think of being *shameless* in only negative terms: someone with no social awareness or sense of common decorum, someone with no fear of God and no concern for others. And while that alarming aspect of our culture is growing by leaps and bounds, *shameless* also has positive attributes: *unconcealed, undisguised, transparent, unashamed.*[3]

Jesus invites us into His presence without shame, without our past baggage, without the need to cover ourselves or to be someone we're not, without the enemy's constant taunts in our ear telling us we're not enough, and without the self-deprecating slurs we constantly hurl at ourselves. He wants us in His presence, full and free, healed and whole, expectant and full of faith.

Jesus wants to heal us deeply so we'll more readily believe that He loves us completely. And when we start to grasp how secure we are in Him, we'll be more apt to pray and believe from *that* sturdy place. We'll learn to trust His promises, rely on His goodness, and rest on His unchanging grace.

The less shame has its hold on us, the more bravely and boldly we'll dare to pray. Of course, this doesn't mean we ever dictate to God. But it does mean we get to have constant and continual conversations *with* God. And our appeal means so much to God that He moves and answers in a way that is completely and totally disproportionate to who we are or to what we could ever dream to accomplish on our own. Let us, therefore, come boldly before the Throne of Grace, excited, assured, expectant, and full of joy. We belong to a sovereign, good, kind, powerful, and loving Father who doesn't treat us as our sinfulness warrants. He loves us with a power and a grace that changes us from an orphan to an heir. May we finally live and believe and pray and breathe like it's true. Because it is.

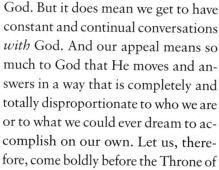

God wants us in His presence, full and free, healed and whole, expectant and full of faith.

A Blessing for You

May you look around and notice all of the answers to prayer you enjoy because of prayers you prayed some time ago. May the breakthroughs you've experienced and the open doors you've walked through compel you to pray with more fervency, specificity, and tenacity. God loves your faith. He loves your heart. He loves it when you pray. He's very protective of you and won't give you something that's not good for you. He makes you wait because He's making you ready. Trust your whole soul and story to

Him. And keep praying. God continues to move in your life, even when you can't see it. One day, your faith will become sight. A blessed, beautiful, and prayerful day to you today!

Let's Pray . . .

Precious Lord, I come to You today humbly aware of how much I miss because I doubt Your love and goodness toward me. Heal me, Lord, in the deepest places of my soul, heal me and make me whole so that I can love deeply and believe profoundly in Your promises. You are God Most High, and You delight in me. You put the stars in place and You care about me! Father, move everything out of my life that keeps me from knowing You in a way that changes me. Awaken fresh faith and persistence in me so I can come humbly and boldly before You. Blow Your Spirit-wind in my sails so I will pray and not give up, so I will seek and not let up, and so I will knock and not give up. When You look for faith on the earth, may You find it in me. In Jesus' matchless, mighty name, I pray, Amen.

Praying God's Word

Write out a personalized prayer and weave in the truths of the following Scripture. Make the declaration that no matter what you're facing right now, nothing can separate you from the love of God!

Let us then approach God's throne of grace with confidence, so that we may receive mercy and find grace to help us in our time of need.

Hebrews 4:16

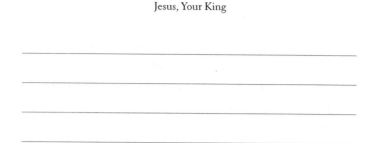

A POWERFUL WORD: *Keep Knocking!*

Sometimes we're afraid of praying for miracles because we're afraid that God won't answer, but the answer isn't up to us. We never know if the answer will be yes, no, or not yet. But the answer isn't up to us. It's not our job to answer; it's our job to ask. And Jesus exhorts us to ask. "Ask and it will be given to you; seek and you will find; knock and the door will be opened to you." These three words—ask, seek, and knock—are present imperative verbs. In other words, they aren't something we do once; they are actions that are repeated over and over and over again. Keep asking. Keep seeking. Keep knocking.[4]

Personal Reflection

1. Do you have a certain past experience that continues to plague and accuse you? Write down the impact those accusations have had on you. Sometimes just to see them on paper is enough to recognize the enemy's lies for what they are.

2. Now find passages that speak of God's love and forgiveness. Spend time with God, and remind your soul that there is now therefore NO condemnation in you because you belong to Jesus (Romans 8:1). Now, in that very place of defeat, dare to ask God for something audacious!

3. How often do you live with a low level of insecurity or disappointment in yourself? Might that be shame? Ask God to

show you what life experiences opened the door to shame. Dare to trust Him with this process. He's got you.

4. Take time and pray through the passage in 1 John 1:9, and emphasize the word *all* in your prayers. Celebrate your NEW identity in Christ Jesus. Come boldly before God and thank Him for ALL you possess in Him. (Note: Naming the blessings one by one will strengthen your soul.)

5. Do you tend to persist in prayer or give up after a short time? Ask God to show you what He wants you to ask Him for, what He invites you to believe Him for. Then write it down, persist in prayer, and do not give up. He is faithful to His word.

6. Do you need God to defend your reputation? Do you long for Him to vindicate you? Remember the parable of the widow and the unrighteous judge. Psalm 62:7 says this: "My salvation and my honor depend on God; he is my mighty rock, my refuge." Remember, if you can trust Him with your eternity, you can trust Him with your honor here on earth. Write down a prayer declaring your trust in God in this place.

7. Has the enemy stolen something from you that you want back? Approach the Throne of Grace. Ask. Seek. Knock. And keep at it. Ask God to give you battle strategy for how to pray, how to stand, and what to believe Him for regarding this battle. Spend some time in Psalm 18; it'll strengthen your heart.

Group Reflection

1. Can you identify any "pockets" of shame in your life? Places where the enemy has held you back or kept you from going after God's promises? Share if you feel comfortable.

2. How often do you entertain self-defeating, self-depre-cating thoughts? How do those thoughts impact your perspective on prayer and on your heir status?

3. Are there areas of your prayer life that feel unhindered—times when you feel bold and audacious, persistent and prayerful? Share about those.

4. If you've identified areas where you're less apt to pray boldly, share those, and tell why you feel stuck (e.g., per-haps it feels noble *not to* ask for certain things).

5. Remember what James 4:3 says? We have not because we ask not, and when we do ask, we ask with the wrong mo-tives. So this is not to say that anything goes in our prayer lives, but it is to say that we let a lot of *God-invitations* fall by the wayside because we misinterpret shame for humility or nobility. I dare you to dig deeper on this one.

6. Spend some time praying for soul-healing so that shame will no longer hinder your prayer life or keep you from an honest, confident, joyful relationship with the Father.

7. Take some time, go around the room, and share words of encouragement with one another. What do you see in someone else (that they may not see in themselves)? May God help you reflect His heart to someone in your group today.

12

Dare to Dream

Expect to Persevere

No matter how fierce the fight or how long the night, He is the only One worth trusting when the chips are down. He will never fail or forsake you. The God Who Fights For You can be trusted with the details of your life, your love, and your battles. Trust Him.

Bo Stern, *Ruthless*

Now to him who is able to do immeasurably more than all we ask or imagine, according to his power that is at work within us, to him be glory in the church and in Christ Jesus throughout all generations, for ever and ever! Amen.

Ephesians 3:20–21

About six months ago, my hubby and I decided to step up our prayer life and zero in on some very specific areas where we longed to see God's influence and movement. We already had an active prayer life, but we sensed God's invitation to lean in, press in, and seek Him more purposefully for the concerns of our hearts. We wrote down six areas of life, committed them to earnest prayer, and asked God to work, move, and do the *impossible*. We engaged in this prayer exercise with energy and expectancy. We asked God to bring about accelerated freedom, power, and movement in the following areas:

- our children
- our extended family
- our community
- the persecuted and poor
- our ministry
- our finances

Every morning and every night we appealed to the God of heaven to do great, accelerated, noticeable things in direct response to our prayers. We wrote down specific requests and found verses in Scripture to anchor us upward.

About a week and a half after we started this purposeful pursuit, all hell broke loose in our family.

Out of the blue, my son received word from his wife letting him know she wanted out of their almost-three-year marriage. Within a moment's notice, our young adult son moved out of the home he and his wife owned together, and moved in with us with only a few of his belongings. One of which was an utterly broken heart. He struggled for healing and answers. I felt stunned by the suddenness of it all.

The next week we received a call that our dear niece was in a life-threatening tubing accident and was on a life-flight from a Wisconsin hospital to the University of Minnesota hospital. The week after that, we received word that doctors found thirty more tumors in my brother's bladder at his cancer recheck appointment.

The following week my other brother and his wife (parents of the niece in the tubing accident) admitted their college-age son to the U of M hospital with what turned out to be ulcerative colitis. Over the next couple of months he'd end up needing four blood transfusions. And *several* times over those same months, my brother and his wife would have those two kids in the same hospital at the same time.

We were in continual communication via text. Daily I'd receive texts like, "They're doing a chemo bladder wash to treat Greg's cancer. Tony is back in for more blood work and Kelsey is on her way to X-ray now. How's Jordan?"

Losing our daughter-in-law felt like a death in the family. Watching my brokenhearted son sort through the shock of it all left me breathless. My heart, prayers, and thoughts were consumed with not only our own heartbreak, but also with the thought that we could have lost our dear niece, or that my nephew could lose his colon, or that my brother would have another cancer fight on his hands.

We came together and prayed more earnestly as brothers and sisters, aunts and uncles, than we ever had before. I sent out morning devotional texts, and other siblings shared verses or thoughts in the group text. The days turned into weeks, which turned to months. Though we had heartbreaking, discouraging days, we also watched as God worked and we deeply sensed His presence in our midst. We banded together as a family and put a flag of faith in the ground. Though we couldn't quite make sense of it all, we truly knew that God was *with us* in our storm.

We eagerly anticipated a family wedding coming up at the end of the summer. We all desperately needed to laugh and dance and celebrate the blessings we still enjoyed. We had each other and we had our faith, which, we knew firsthand, was being refined and strengthened in the fire.

Two weeks prior to the wedding, we received a frantic text from my sister, the mother of the bride-to-be. My sister was headed to the ER with her hubby, who was experiencing abdominal pain. We couldn't believe it, given everything else going on, but once again we looked to God together and we prayed.

My sister's next text rocked our world. Doctors found a mass on Donny's pancreas. Turned out to be inoperable cancer. My thoughts raced and my heart ached for Krissy, my baby sister. She and Donny had dated since they were young teenagers. He's as much my brother as she is my sister. They're only in their forties. Krissy's thoughts were on repeat: *I'm too young to be a widow. I still want to be a wife.*

We were all absolutely undone by this news. For two weeks we reeled, we grieved, we prayed, we hoped. And we prepared for the wedding.

Though I went to work every day to do my live talk radio show, I always felt on the verge of tears, as my heart grieved over so many things. And yet, as Kev and I worked our way through our prayer list every day and every night, we felt more grounded in Christ than ever. We were anchored to His promises. And though the winds continued to blow, we still sensed God's invitation to find Him here and to watch Him move.

Looking back, I think God invited us to up our game because He knew we'd need it in order to stand.

Treasures in the Darkness

My original deadline for this book was mid-August, smack dab in the middle of all of these crises. My publisher graciously offered me a five-month extension. So here I sit in January, with far more insight than I had in August.

We're still praying for a miracle for my brother-in-law Donny. I'm so praying that he'll still be with us by the time this book actually releases. My brother Greg continues to work his way through his treatment, but things look good. Kelsey and Tony are both on the mend and learning to live with some of the issues that still plague them. And Jordan is becoming the man of God we always prayed he would be, raised him to be. He's seeking God, reading the Word, and determined never again to put anything but Jesus at the center of his life.

Quite a number of our nieces and nephews have engaged their faith on a deeper level from this summer's battle. One of my nephews sent me a text that read something like, *"Hey, Auntie Susie, this is your favorite nephew. I just wanted to tell you that I've decided to trust God with my life. I got down on my knees at work and surrendered my life to Christ. I just wanted you to know."* I held my phone to my chest, absolutely undone, in the best way.

As a family, we are clinging to God's promises on a whole new level. And guess what? We're. Still. Standing.

And Kevin and I? Every which way we turn we see answers to our earnest prayers spring up all around us. Our faith has become sight. We're more convinced than ever that not only has God been working in our midst (as evidenced by the many answers we see before us), He's working still, in deeper ways that we cannot see or fathom right now. So we engage our faith. We're not shrinking back. We're stepping up and we're asking for *more*.

God, will You move in our family in a way that forever marks the way we all walk with You? May we each encounter You in a heart-rending, soul-stirring way that forever changes how we relate to You and how we walk out our days on this earth. And will You move in our community in surprising and miraculous ways? May the lost be found, the sick healed, and the broken restored! And will You perform wonders and miracles among our persecuted brothers and sisters, in such an awe-inspiring way that many will see and hear and put their trust in the name of our God? May our brothers and sisters in these desperate places, and their oppressors, know—beyond a shadow of a doubt—that there's a God in heaven who works wonders for His children! And God, will You help us pay off our mortgage quickly and proficiently so we can give away more and more to those in need? Father, put audacious vision and courageous faith in our hearts! Help us to believe You for the impossible, help us to attempt the unachievable, and help us to have faith to receive the unbelievable, straight from Your hands. We're done shrinking back in self-protection. You are mighty to save and You mean what You say. So we stand with outstretched arms and pray: God, hear our prayers and do wonders in our midst!

In the matchless name of Jesus, we pray, Amen.

There's no battle, no scheme, no attack of the enemy that can keep us from God's love, His presence, and His power. And our trials will always serve us, teach us, and strengthen us in the end.

> I will go before you and will level the mountains;
> I will break down gates of bronze and cut through bars
>   of iron.
> I will give you hidden treasures, riches stored in secret
>   places,
> so that you may know that I am the Lord,
> the God of Israel, who summons you by name.
>
> Isaiah 45:2–3

Persevering prayer is not for the faint of heart. It's far easier to give up than it is to go forward. It's much easier to complain than it is to contend. Griping about our circumstances is natural.

Grabbing hold of promises that defy our circumstances? Well, that's gritty and *super*natural.

Sometimes prayer feels like the most delightful, intimate fellowship with God, but other times it feels like we're fighting alone with hands bloodied from battle, and it's all we can do to hold on to what God has promised us.

But given the times we're in, don't you think we *need* to learn to prevail in prayer? When it's delightful and when it feels like a bloody battle? When God is giving us what we want and when He calls us to pray and intercede for what *He* wants?

Culture seems to be imploding all around us. Evil is on the rise. Selfish people are celebrated while reverent people are mocked. If we look too long at the stats or our circumstances, we can start to wonder if we're on the losing side.

But remember? We win in the end! Yet even right now, the enemy baits us into one of two ditches:

- To shake our fist at the darkness and hate those who defy our God and all that we hold sacred
- To put our head in the sand and entertain ourselves to death so we don't have to face the challenging times we're in

Both of these options please our natural flesh-tendency, but they're slippery slopes that pull us right into disobedience. God calls us to love our enemies and to pray for those who want to hurt us. He also charges us to be focused and alert, prayerful and sober, discerning of the times so we'll know what to do.

We're free to walk with Christ in a marginal way (with huge consequences, of course), or in a purposeful, profound way.

We're saved by grace. But we're *invited* to become spiritually agile and prayerfully powerful in a way that transforms us and changes the world. But this process *always* calls for perseverance. Here's an important point for all of us to remember: *Jesus offers us all the resources of heaven, but He doesn't force us to lay hold of them.*

> Do you make big asks of God? Don't be timid in your prayers. Prayer should be as big as God's promises and as full as God's resources. Your requests should require the full power and provision of God.[1]

One day we'll see Jesus face to face, and we'll realize that He meant it when He invited us to enjoy intimate fellowship with Him, day by day and moment by moment. His promises really were *for us.*

In Christ, you have full and legal access to all of the riches in the heavenly realm. You are invited to participate in the Big Story, the Ultimate Games, the Kingdom Showdown. Not as a spectator or as a Monday-morning quarterback, but as an Heir-Warrior-Treasured-Child of God.

Are you willing to go the distance and access *everything* God has made available to you? Will you throw off everything that slows you down and run this race to win? I absolutely love Eugene Peterson's paraphrase of Hebrews 12:1–3:

> Do you see what this means—all these pioneers who blazed the way, all these veterans cheering us on? It means we'd better get on with it. Strip down, start running—and never quit! No extra spiritual fat, no parasitic sins. Keep your eyes on *Jesus,* who both began and finished this race we're in. Study how he did it. Because he never lost sight of where he was headed—that exhilarating finish in and with God—he could put up with anything along the way: Cross, shame, whatever. And now he's *there,* in the place of honor, right alongside God. When you find yourselves flagging in your faith, go over that story again, item by item, that long litany of hostility he plowed through. *That* will shoot adrenaline into your souls!

How Much Do You Want Him?

It's fun to cast vision and make lofty goals based on fresh ideas. It's inspiring to stand on our tippy-toes and imagine where our dreams might take us. But it's truly grueling to walk out the process in the daily grind. This ferocious faith journey is not for sissies, and it's why so few persevere and go on to believe for and see great fruit that actually outlives them. Yet that's exactly what Jesus has anointed and appointed us for:

> You did not choose me, but I chose you and appointed you so that you might go and bear fruit—fruit that will last—and so that whatever you ask in my name the Father will give you.
>
> John 15:16

Notice in the verse above how Jesus connected fruit that outlives us with prayers that go beyond us. Why do you suppose He made that connection? What would happen if more of us took God at His Word? What would change in us and around us if we were less apt to be so quickly discouraged and derailed from that ancient path of faith? What if an army of us rose up this very hour and decided to lean forward, run hard, and believe God *for more*?

What is more glorious than God's presence, or more potent than His promises? What compares to the beauty of His creation and the majesty of His handiwork? Nothing. Not. A. Thing.

Is there a loftier goal or worthier pursuit than Jesus Himself? Who is better than Jesus? Who compares to Him? Has anyone loved us with such pure devotion or profound redemption? Does anyone have the power to wipe away our sin, transform our hearts, secure our future, and redeem our stories? Nobody *but* Jesus. Not. A. One.

Jesus is our King and so worthy of our lives, our prayers, our dreams, and our endurance. We live and breathe today for Him.

Care For Your Soul, Then Re-engage

I've just come through a second-mile season. You know, the part of the journey that feels long, lonely, windy, and just hard. All of the painful family crises broke my heart. Fault-finding, nit-picky Christians burdened my mind and drained my soul. And the daily demands of work and home left me just downright weary.

I decided to change up my prayer focus. I put myself in a Jesus-eclipse. Let me explain. I took my weary self and drew ever closer to Jesus. I scooted up so close to Him that my only heart's cry was for more of Him *in* me. I knew I couldn't manage all that weighed so heavily on me, so I gave Him every shred of it. I gave Him the deep burdens that plagued our family. I entrusted ministry outcomes and opportunities to His care. I even handed over the stone-throwers and the rock-stackers, trusting He could better deal with them than I could. I stopped praying about everything and anything except Him.

This for me was a new place of abiding. A place where the Main Thing upstaged every other peripheral thing. I hid myself in Jesus, with no thoughts or wants other than Jesus. And it was good. For a time.

Then one day I recorded an interview with singer-songwriter Wintley Phipps. This man has prayerfully cultivated a lifestyle of listening and response. He aims to be continually in step with Jesus so he'll be available for however Jesus wants to use him.

For example, one day Wintley boarded a train and noticed a man with his head down. The guy looked dejected and burdened. His papers and briefcase spilled onto the seat next to him, which sent the message that he'd rather sit alone.

Feeling nudged by the Spirit, Wintley couldn't help himself. He asked, "Excuse me, sir, is this seat taken?" Wintley then sat down next to a man who didn't want company but desperately needed a friend. Guess who that man was? Charles Colson.

God planted divine friendship seeds that day. Wintley went on to serve alongside Chuck Colson in prison ministry for almost twenty years. All birthed out of that "chance" meeting that Wintley could have missed had he not been willing to listen or respond.

Another time while on a flight to an engagement, Wintley noticed a flight attendant who seemed noticeably burdened. He sensed the nudge to reach out to her and speak a word of encouragement to her. He pulled out a cassette tape (remember those?) of his music and offered it to her. "I pray this encourages you in the days to come." She smiled, admitted she'd been having a tough time, and thanked Wintley.

Three days later she felt the nudge to share that cassette tape with another man on her flight. She approached him and said, "Sir? Have you ever heard of a young man named Wintley Phipps?" "Why no, I haven't," the man replied. She continued, "This music has been a blessing to me, but I want you to have it now."

The man on the plane that day was Cliff Barrows, Billy Graham's right-hand man and music director. Three weeks later, Wintley received a call from Cliff, who invited him to become a soloist for the Billy Graham crusades. Wintley served with the Billy Graham Evangelistic Association for the next twenty-five years.

Wintley shared one supernatural "coincidence" story after another. My heart pitter-pattered as I listened.

Here is my paraphrase of what he shared in that deep, baritone voice of his: "Susie, these are moments of destiny that are available to *all* of God's children. Nothing happens by chance, and if we make ourselves available to the Lord, He'll open doors and connect us with people we would never otherwise meet. He *wants* to open doors and provide opportunities to use us for His grand purpose. But here's a very important point: these divine moments aren't our full and true destiny. They're not what we're ultimately made for. Our true destiny is this: *To be transformed into the image of Christ. And yet, these moments are significant parts of our story and we can celebrate them and trust God to orchestrate them.* God is in the miracle-working business, and He will use every circumstance, every hardship, every divine connection to remind us that He is God, He loves us, and He intends to make us more like Him."

Jesus calls me to the sacred race that requires an active prayer life, thick skin, a tender heart, a love for the unlovely, and a willingness to persevere.

I knew this truth in my head. And even in my heart. But I realized at that moment that it was time for me to get back in the game. My time of hiddenness had turned into a time of self-protection.

I needed a fresh reminder that though Jesus is my hiding place, He calls me to the sacred race that requires an active prayer life, thick skin, a tender heart, a love for the unlovely, and a willingness to persevere.

My heart's cry is that you and I will embrace such an engaged, expectant faith that divine coincidences and chance meetings become a regular occurrence for us.

Glimpses Now, Glory Later

The prayers of the Christ-follower move heaven and change things on earth. Our presence and our prayers impact and influence the greater kingdom story. Isn't that amazing?

Scripture repeatedly speaks of the power of prayer and of God's willingness to move when we appeal to Him. Yet obviously, we don't always receive what we ask for. And oftentimes, after the fact, we realize that's a good thing, because while we may know what we want, we don't always know what we need. And God is only interested in giving His children the best things, for His glory, and for our goodness.

Yet sometimes we may hit the bull's-eye with our prayers and still not see an answer to those prayers in this life. In my younger years, I'd read passages like Hebrews 11, where it says that some of the saints who've gone before us never received what was promised them. And I'd wonder, what was the point of prayer if it wouldn't change my circumstance in this life? If they received a promise, shouldn't they receive that which was promised them?

My perspective has changed over the years. I've walked with God long enough to know that He is a good, good Father. And He withholds *no* good thing from those who walk intimately with Him. I've come to understand how brief our lives on earth really are.

Life is short. Eternity is long. And if God makes us wait for an answer, it's because the answer isn't temporary. It's eternal. And when we see all He's prepared for us, we'll wonder why we ever doubted Him in the first place. He is a promise maker and a promise keeper. It's impossible for Him to fail us.

But gratefully, He answers many of our prayers in our life-time. New jobs, relationships restored, financial provision, open doors, and so on. He hears us when we call on Him. He remembers even when we forget. He never forgets. He's always faithful. He opens the heavens, parts the waters, and gives us glimpses of glory now so we can trust Him with the fullness of our story.

> From his abundance we have all received one gracious blessing after another.
>
> John 1:16 NLT

May we be wise enough to see life more as a marathon than a sprint. May we take good care of our hearts and purposefully nourish our faith. And may we refuse the extremes of demanding things from God, or doubting that He cares. May we instead walk the narrow road of holiness, humility, perseverance, and expectancy because *we know* that our posture, our perspective, and our prayers make all the difference in the world.

Life is short. Eternity is long. And if God makes us wait for an answer, it's because the answer isn't temporary. It's eternal.

God is powerful and active on the earth today. He's not asleep. He has not looked away. He's very much involved with this chapter of the kingdom story.

And when He searches the world over, looking for faith in the hearts of men, may He be pleased to find *great faith* in you.

> It is written: "I believed; therefore I have spoken." Since we have that same spirit of faith, we also believe and therefore speak, because we know that the one who raised the Lord Jesus from the dead will also raise us with Jesus and present us with you to himself. All this is for your benefit, so that the grace that is reaching more and more people may cause thanksgiving to overflow to the glory of God.
>
> Therefore we do not lose heart. Though outwardly we are wasting away, yet inwardly we are being renewed day by day. For our light and momentary troubles are achieving for us an eternal glory that far outweighs them all. So we fix our eyes not on what is seen, but on what is unseen, since what is seen is temporary, but what is unseen is eternal.
>
> 2 Corinthians 4:13–18

What a treasured honor it's been to make this journey with you. Oh, I pray that we, as God's people, grow more passionate and purposeful with each passing day. This is not our home!

We're only passing through. But how we live *here* impacts how we live *there*—in heaven—where we'll forever abide with our Savior and King. You are His treasured, holy possession, and He will see that you get safely home. Praise His holy name forever.

~Susie Larson

A Blessing for You

May you become an expert at caring for your soul. May you know when to tuck yourself under the shadow of God's wing and when to run to the battle line, knowing He'll fight for you. May you know when to rest and know when to work. May you refuse worry and embrace faith instead. May you guard against toxic thoughts, attitudes, and mind-sets that only weaken you. May you instead fill your thoughts with all that's lovely, praiseworthy, and true. In the days ahead, may your intimate walk with Jesus inform your decisions, fuel your prayers, and magnify your love. May Jesus fill you up to overflowing from one moment to the next. Have a wise and winsome day today!

Let's Pray . . .

Lord, I know You are on the move, answering prayers and the cries of my heart. I say thank You, by faith, for the answers that are already on their way. You always keep Your word and stay true to Your promises. Thank You, dear Lord, for Your faithfulness to me. Help me not to live a small, selfish life. I long to stay engaged in the sacred race You've appointed for me. I believe that stunning surprises and startling breakthroughs lie ahead for me. These glimpses of glory and moments of destiny are mine because I'm Yours. I know they don't make up my whole story. My story, my song, is to praise Your name, to become like You, and to walk intimately with You all the days of my life. So I hold fast to You, and I look expectantly for a breakthrough. Since You won't forget Your Word, neither will I! I will embrace Your promises with perseverance, expectancy, tenacity, and hope. You are a miracle-working God and You are working wonders in me. Fill me afresh with the wonder of Your great love. Help me to live and breathe and pray and work in a manner worthy of Your name. In Your matchless name I pray, Amen.

Praying God's Word

Write out a personalized prayer and weave in the truths of the following Scripture. Make the declaration that no matter what you're facing right now, nothing can separate you from the love of God!

Therefore we do not lose heart. Though outwardly we are wasting away, yet inwardly we are being renewed day by day. For our light and momentary troubles are achieving for us an eternal glory that far outweighs them all. So we fix our eyes not on what is seen, but on what is unseen, since what is seen is temporary, but what is unseen is eternal.

2 Corinthians 4:16–18

_____

_____

_____

_____

A POWERFUL WORD: *Soldier On!*

So walk on, child of God. You shall not go down, you shall not be defeated, you shall not be overtaken, God is with you. So walk on. He brings you through the water, through the river and through the fire because He has a greater purpose for you on the other side: no matter what you face, God is going to get some glory. Whenever you experience tough times, the Spirit of the living God will press the rewind button, and His voice will remind you that you have His word to walk you through *anything*. He created you. He redeemed you. He paid the price and you are His. So *walk on!*[2]

Personal Reflection

1. What is God saying to you about your own heart, perspective, and faith in this particular season of life? Are you hiding and abiding? Or are you self-protecting and rejecting the notion that God has *more* for you?

2. What do you need most right now? Is it rest, time in God's Word, a reframed perspective, a friend to remind you what's true, or something else entirely? Write it down and ask God for provision and direction.

3. What do you know to be true about prayer, God, and His faithfulness that you didn't know (or didn't know as deeply) prior to your most recent storm or battle?

4. Think back to times that you earnestly prayed and God gave you a peek into His movement in your life. How did those glimpses of His handiwork encourage your heart and impact your prayers? Write down a few specific instances that come to mind.

5. Pause for a moment and take inventory of your current life season. Where do you see God's involvement in your story in even the slightest way? Try not to be so obsessed

with the big breakthroughs that you miss the small blessings and breakthroughs. Most answers to prayer come one puzzle piece at a time.

6. After counting your blessings and thanking God for His very real involvement in your life, look up and ask for eyes to see what He's up to all around you. Ask Him for more faith and more passion to pray His promises and trust His faithfulness.

7. Though it's tempting to keep ourselves in the smaller story, God continually beckons us to participate in the greater kingdom story. As far as you can discern, describe what your greater role might be in the story God continues to write on the earth today.

Group Reflection

1. What is God saying to you these days?

2. When you consider your current season and battles, what do wisdom and faith require of you right now?

3. Take your time and think about this one: What's the next wise step for you? How can you engage or re-engage your faith with a greater level of expectancy?

4. Why do you suppose God allows us to persevere at times beyond what we think we can handle? What does perseverance develop in us? (Hint: see James 1.)

5. In your opinion, why do so few Christians dream big dreams? Why do fewer still persevere through the process?

6. What's the ripple effect or the impact on the body of Christ if too many Christians live dreamless, mundane, disengaged lives? Answer this one as thoughtfully as you're able.

7. Spend some time praying for the body of Christ, that we might rise up in faith, dare to dream, and be willing to persevere.

Sample Prayers

Expect to be challenged. The enemy won't go down without a fight. But expect great progress. Life is different on the west side of the Jordan. Breakthroughs outnumber breakdowns. God's promises outweigh personal problems. Victory becomes, dare we imagine, a way of life. Isn't it time for you to change your mailing address from the wilderness to the Promised Land? Your Glory Days await you. Ready to march?

Max Lucado, *Glory Days*

The path of the righteous is like the morning sun, shining ever brighter till the full light of day.

Proverbs 4:18

Let's get a vision for where God is taking us and what God wants for us. We stand in the midst of a fierce battle with an enemy whose aim is to rob us blind, kill any evidence of budding life or potential growth, and destroy any hope or dream God gives us. But we serve a God who means what He says, who does what He promises to do, and who will one day put that enemy in his proper place.

Until then, let us take God at His word. Let us learn to stand in battle. Let us persevere in prayer. And may the battles and the blessings in our lives transform us from strength to strength, glory to glory, that we may shine ever brighter until the full light of day.

Here are just a few sample prayers to help you if you need them. Start a journal of your own prayers. Find passages of Scripture that speak to your heart. In the days to come, that battle plan of yours will become a most sacred possession.

The Lord's Prayer

I pray the Lord's Prayer almost every morning during my quiet time. Being the visual person that I am, I often picture myself among an endless throng of believers, looking at our King up on a high cliff. (I can't help but picture something like the scene of Simba's birth in *The Lion King*.) Think about this for a moment: God knows you intimately, profoundly, as a one-of-a-kind individual. And He knows me in the same intimate, profound way. He delights in *every* detail of our lives. He hears us when we pray. And though we're unique in ourselves, we're one of many. When we picture ourselves among the many who belong to Jesus, we remember that we're part of a much greater kingdom story. And though our part is divinely important, it's not more or less significant than another's role in this same story. The thought of being divinely known as one, yet profoundly one of many, keeps us humble and hopeful, grateful, and grounded. And the idea of appealing to almighty God that His kingdom might be established on earth as it is in heaven, well, it makes me tremble. So let's pray . . .

> Our Father in heaven,
> hallowed be your name,
> your kingdom come,

200

your will be done,
on earth as it is in heaven.
Give us today our daily bread.
And forgive us our debts,
as we also have forgiven our debtors.
And lead us not into temptation,
but deliver us from the evil one.

Matthew 6:9–13

For Thine is the kingdom, and the power, and the glory, both now and forevermore.

I Am Yours, You Are Mine

Sometimes—right in the middle of our difficult circumstances—we need to put a flag in the ground and declare God's faithfulness to us and our commitment to Him. Here's a prayer to get you started . . .

Father in heaven, I want to pause and tell You how great You are. You are God Most High—towering above my circumstances, above my fears, and above my dreams. You are the star-breathing God so vast, so great—and yet so close, intimately right here, right now. I'd rather be a doorkeeper in Your house than a big deal anywhere else. I am Yours and You are mine. Your banner over me is love. Just wanted to declare Your greatness today. Thank You for saving and redeeming my life. I will follow You forever, Amen.

A Hard Day's Night

If you've had a rough day and you find yourself weary and worn out at night, it's good to wrap up your day with thoughts of God's faithfulness. He is an ever-present help in times of trouble. He cares about the deepest longings of our hearts. And He'll carry burdens that feel too heavy for us to carry. Let's pray . . .

Lord, what a day it's been. I've seen Your goodness and glory, and I've taken a few arrows that have left me burdened and breathless. But You are still God. You are on Your throne. You will see me through. You will take what the enemy meant for evil and turn it for good. I hide myself in the shadow of Your wing. I entrust my soul to You, knowing You have me on Your heart and in Your hand. Tonight I will rest in You, Amen.

And here's another one . . .

Lord, I'm weary after a long day. I lift my chin and look to You. I offer You the cares from the day, the concerns of my heart, and the things that keep me up at night. Take my sincere yet imperfect offerings and miraculously multiply them to meet the needs around me. When I crawl under the covers tonight, help me to remember that I'm not under my circumstances. I'm safe under the shadow of Your wing. Cover me with sweet, nourishing sleep tonight. Oh, how I love You. Amen.

Prayer for Your Family

Every one of our families needs God's involvement and God's answers. If you feel especially burdened these days with the needs within your family, here's a prayer to get you started . . .

Precious Lord, pour out Your Spirit on this amazing family of mine. Each and every one of them. Thank You for loving us with an everlasting love. Heal us in mind, body, and spirit! Awaken our faith! Empower our prayers! Engage our hearts! Help us to see what You want us to see, say what You want us to say, and pray what You want to pray. We belong to You. We are Your ambassadors on the earth today. You are good. Your promises are true, and You will make a way for us. We lift our hands in praise for all You've done and all You have yet to do. You are always good and we are always loved. Thank You, Jesus, Amen

A Renewed Perspective

I don't know about you, but my perspective can go south in about ten seconds flat. If I dwell on my fears, or my physical symptoms, or the meanness of people, my emotions will lead me right into the ditch. But when I look above those things to the One who will most certainly have the last say, peace returns and with it, my perspective. If that describes you too, maybe this prayer will encourage you today . . .

Lord Jesus, glorify Your name in me—in my wins and my losses, in my heartaches and my joys. Be my strength today. Be the song of my heart and the reason that I sing. Lift me up so I can see things from Your perspective. Strengthen me to stand right here, right now, while I wait for my breakthroughs and celebrate my victories. You are alive in me. My heart cannot even fathom the good things You have in store for me. Help me to live with my spirit-eyes open so that my heart beats in rhythm with Yours. Any gift from Your hand pales in comparison to knowing Your heart. You're my greatest treasure, and I embrace wholehearted faith this day!

Abundantly Equipped

I pray this prayer for my family almost daily. It's based mainly on Philippians 1:9–11, 20:

> *Lord Jesus, may our love abound more and more. May we increase daily in all wisdom, knowledge, and depth of insight. May we understand the times and know what to do. May we be high discerners of Your will, Your wisdom, and Your truth. May we walk purely and blamelessly before You that our lives will honor You in both life and death. And may we ever and always bear the fruit of righteousness.*

My Calling, God's Way

I wrote the following prayer based on Romans 4 and have mentioned it in some of my past books and DVDs, but it's worth repeating here. If you struggle with believing God wants to do great things for you, and if you tend to put more confidence in your obstacles than you do His promises, this one is for you . . .

> *Lord, by faith I pray Your promises and make this declaration over my life:*
>
> *Without weakening in my faith, I will face the fact that there are many reasons I should not be able to fulfill the call of God on my life. But I will not waver in unbelief regarding the promises of God! No, I will be strengthened in my faith, giving glory to God because I am fully persuaded that GOD has the power to do what He has promised. Therefore, I will put no confidence in my obstacles because I've put all of my hope in the power, and the authority, and the faithfulness of almighty God who daily establishes His purposes for me!*

Faith Amidst Disappointment

Oftentimes when we walk through seasons of disappointment, we forget to look for the treasures hidden in those circumstances. God allows nothing He can't use for His glory and for our goodness. He doesn't cause heartbreak, but He'll most certainly use it if we let Him. Look for glimpses of His goodness in your current season of life. They're there.

Precious Father, how wonderful You are! Thank You for loving me like You do. You are showing me how to find high ground even in the valley of disappointment. I now see this phase of my journey as sacred and significant. Help me to look for and find the treasures in this place. This I know: You are changing me, transforming me into Your likeness. I am living and breathing on the earth today to bring You glory and reflect Your goodness. And no delay or disappointment can keep me from that divine appointment! Continue Your good work in me. Thank You for all of the blessings I enjoy today. Help me never take them for granted. I love You, Jesus, Amen.

Be Uncommon

Every single day we're faced with options of judgment or mercy, pride or humility, pettiness or honor, gossip or intercession. Years ago I wrote a book titled *The Uncommon Woman*. Here's a prayer from that book. It's the cry of my heart. May it be yours too.

Precious Lord, I ask Your forgiveness for every time I've chosen pettiness over prayer. Forgive me for so easily giving in to catty thoughts and useless words. I long to be an uncommon woman. I am an uncommon woman! Fill me

205

afresh with a sense of Your love and holiness. Compel me to walk in a more noble way. Draw me to prayer. Speak to me when I'm there. And help me listen. I want to change the world by the way I live. Thank You for leaving me with such a tangible example of what true and humble love looks like. Continue Your good work in me. In Your name, I pray, Amen.[1]

For Your Prodigal

Just as John expressed in 3 John 4, "I have no greater joy than to hear that my children are walking in the truth," there's truly no greater sorrow when our children aren't walking in the truth that will set them free. While a couple of my sons didn't outright reject their faith, for several seasons in a row, they wandered away from a close, engaged relationship with Jesus and into the ways of the world. That was enough to break my heart. I learned to pray not only for my own broken heart but also for the countless moms and dads who knew a pain even deeper than mine. Maybe that's you. If so, let's pray . . .

Precious Lord, here I am again, lifting up my loved ones to You. Jesus, draw them near, by the power of Your Holy Spirit. Heal their deepest wounds. Make their crooked ways straight. And open their eyes where they are blind. Dear God, drive a wedge between every person and circumstance that the enemy is using to send a lying message to them. Line their path with people and circumstances that speak life-giving, soul-restoring truth until they're totally free! May a revival break out all over our nation! May the prodigals come home, may the weary be restored, and the broken be healed. We wait for You, God, to do what only You can do. You hear us when we pray. Help every brokenhearted mom and dad to rest in the promise that You love our loved one far more passionately than we do! And may we trust You so deeply in this process that we're able to choose joy in the meantime. In Jesus' name, I pray, Amen.

And here's another one . . .

Lord of heaven, hear my earnest plea! Overwhelm my loved ones with Your presence, conviction, and love! Align them with Your divine purposes for them. Jesus, do what only You can do: encounter them, woo them, draw them, protect them, and establish them in Your highest and best purposes for them. With the authority of Christ in me, I condemn the works of the enemy against my children! I stand in the gap and command the forces of evil to stand down. I command unrighteousness to shut its mouth! And with my sword of the Lord, I cut off and cut down every scheme of the enemy, every one of his attempts to derail my children. Lord, protect them from life-altering mistakes and missteps. Lead them not into temptation and deliver them from evil! Give them godly friends and high discernment. Give them strength to walk away from bad influences. Provide godly mentors and great employment. And help me, dear Lord, to walk through this difficult season with strength, favor, and grace. In Jesus' precious, powerful name, I pray, Amen.

Worn and Weary

When we feel the wear and tear of living life in a fallen world, it's good for us to step back and remember that we're not made for this place. We're only passing through. But in the meantime, Jesus promises to renew and refresh us from His bountiful, abundant resources. So let's pray . . .

Father in heaven, heal my soul and make me whole. Help me get to a place where I can rest fully on Your grace, trust fully in Your sovereignty, and rely fully on Your strength— no matter what my eyes see or my emotions tell me. You are good, Your promises are true, and You will always make a way for me. Fill me up to overflowing today. In Your precious name, I pray, Amen.

Affirmation Alphabet

Before you roll your eyes, let me explain. One night I tossed and turned, unable to fall asleep. I had the idea to work my way through the alphabet, naming—by faith—all of the things *I am* because I am *in* Christ Jesus. I challenge you to pick two words per letter and whisper a declaration to your soul (good luck with the letter *X*—I struggled with that one). I will tell you, in the days that followed, I went through this list out loud and came up with additional words. Even today, I find myself praying my way through the alphabet with declarative words that describe my inheritance in Christ Jesus, and I'm always encouraged and inspired afterwards! And it's good brainwork. I'll get you started, but then you take it from here . . .

Thank You, Lord, that I am

A—Anointed and Appointed

B—Blessed and Bold

C—(Full of) Conviction and Compassion

Anchor in the Storm

I don't know anyone right now who isn't either going through a storm, or who loves someone who is. It's easy to forget who

God is to us in the storm. Our souls need reminders now and again. Let's pray . . .

> *I thank You, Jesus, that Your kingdom is sturdier than my circumstances. Your love is more powerful than my blunders. Your power is far more substantial than my strength. And your invitation to rest in You and to be much with You is far more life-giving than any other thing my heart longs for. In You, Lord Jesus, I find the riches my soul longs for and the intimacy I was made for. Help me to find my sturdy and safe place of rest in You today, Amen.*

Make Me Powerful in Prayer

Who doesn't want to be powerful in prayer? Here's a passionate prayer for the one who wants to prevail in prayer. It's my heart's cry. Let's pray . . .

> *Precious and powerful Lord, may the power of Your Holy Spirit fall afresh on me! Hear my prayer and awaken in me fresh and strong compassion, conviction, and love. Fill me with Your grace. Show me my place in the greater kingdom story. May Your clarity and focus be mine. Put power in my prayers and precision in my words. Grant me the tongue of the learned and the tongue of the wise. May I know the word that sustains the weary. May my prayers set captives free! Our nation, our world, is desperate for revival. Dear Lord, raise up an army of intercessors. Deliver the depressed, heal the sick, give clarity to the confused, give strength to the weak, and bring the wayward back home. Release the captives, convict the ignorant, raise up the humble, and humble the proud. Cut off the strength of the wicked and increase the power of the godly. Deliver*

and defend the vulnerable and the weak. And confuse and expose the plans of the wicked. Lord, give us not what we deserve, but what we need. We're desperate for Your mercy and Your grace. Move mightily on the earth today. Move mightily in and through me. In Jesus' name, I pray, Amen.

End-of-Year Prayer

When another year wraps up, it's good for the soul to pause and remember God's goodness. We have a history with God. He's with us in this present moment. And we have a future with Him. He's been good. And He'll be good again. Let's pray . . .

Heavenly Father, as I look back over the year behind me, I thank You that goodness and mercy have followed me every step of the way. As I look ahead to the year before me, I can trust that Your grace will cover me. As I endure the storms that surround me, I know that Your hand will steady me and keep me from going under. I can trust You with every moment of my life, and I'm so grateful. Lead me in Your everlasting way, every single moment of every day. In Your precious name, I pray, Amen.

Acknowledgments

If you read the last chapter of this book you know that I wrote much of this book with a broken heart. Recently I had lunch with my friend Sara Groves, and I shared how the last few months have gone for us. Writing this particular book amidst our family trials has been a practice of utter dependence, which I know is a good thing. Just not always a comfortable thing.

Much like prayer, yes? Prayer involves our willingness to place the weight of our lives on the invisible-yet-tangible faithfulness of Almighty God. It's a practice of utter dependence. And it's not always comfortable. Writing every word of this book has felt exactly that way to me.

Sara sat quietly and listened to me share my heart, and then she replied, "Susie, what kind of book would this have been if you'd written from a place of strength? I think God had you right where He wanted you. You can trust Him." She's right.

While I'll admit I had moments of concern about content and deadlines given the state of things in our family, God consistently and continually gave me grace when I needed it, and I thank Him. May He take this offering and multiply it beyond my wildest dreams. Oh, Lord, let it be so!

I have several others to thank here as well. I pray you'll indulge me for a moment.

Leslie Wilson, thank you for your input, advice, and direction. I'm grateful for your expertise!

Andy McGuire, Carra Carr, Jeff Braun, Shaun Tabatt, and Chandler Smith, thank you for your commitment to this project, to our relationship, and to all things Jesus! I appreciate you so very much. Thank you.

Steve Laube, I've loved working with you. Thank you for understanding my heart and my message like you do. Bless you and thank you.

Dana Ashley and the Ambassador Speakers Bureau, I am ever so grateful for you. Sometimes I feel you get the short end of the stick with me because I have to say *no* more than I can say *yes*, but you always seem to understand. Thank you. Kev and I both appreciate you greatly.

A special thank you to my sample readers who worked their way through each chapter as I wrote it: Bonnie Newberg, Lynn Ferguson, Cindy Larson, Patty Fischer, Kathy Schwanke, Karen Telle, Daryl Jackson, Kay Blake, and Jane Bjork. Thank you, thank you. May God redeem the time you spent reviewing these pages.

To my intercessors: You're always right there when I need you. May Jesus Himself pour life and strength into your soul, and may a fresh awareness of His presence be yours now and always. Thank you.

To my family: My mom, Kev's dad, our siblings, nephews, nieces, and in-laws, I love you. We're in this together. God is with us. May we daily draw near and gain our strength from Him.

To Jake, Lizzie, Luke, Kristen, and Jordan: Time with you all has become one of my most prized possessions. May God continue to work wonders in and through you. I can hardly wait to see how He writes your stories. Dad and I are here, cheering you on and praying passionately, every step of the way.

To my dear, precious husband, Kevin: I love you, honey. You are strong and mighty and true. And so very faithful to God and to me. May each of our sons grow to be men of God just like you are. In the days ahead, may our prayers gain momentum and our faith increase by leaps and bounds!

And finally, and most importantly, to my dear and precious Savior: Jesus, You are the treasure hidden in the everydayness of life. Only the wise will seek after You. And when we find You, we find exactly what our hearts were always made for. That you would allow me to carry Your treasure in this earthen vessel is something I'll never quite comprehend. So grateful to belong to You. Nothing on this earth compares to the treasure and blessing of knowing Your heart. Come quickly, Lord Jesus. We wait for You.

Notes

Introduction

1. Andrew Murray, *Believing Prayer* (Minneapolis: Bethany House, 1980, 2004), 64, emphasis mine.

Chapter 1: Dare to Pray Like You're Loved

1. Susie Larson, *The Uncommon Woman* (Chicago: Moody Publishers, 2008), 18.
2. A.W. Tozer, *The Knowledge of the Holy* (New York: Harper & Row, 1961), 57.
3. Jennifer Kennedy Dean, *Live a Praying Life in Adversity* (Birmingham, AL: New Hope Publishers, 2014), 13.
4. See Romans 8:11
5. See 1 Corinthians 3
6. Andrew Murray, *Believing Prayer* (Minneapolis: Bethany House, 1980, 2004), 45.
7. Lisa Whittle, *I Want God* (Eugene, OR: Harvest House, 2015), 33.

Chapter 2: Dare to Pray for Perspective

1. Warren Wiersbe, *The Wiersbe Bible Commentary* OT (Colorado Springs: David C. Cook, 2007), 478.
2. Ibid., emphasis mine.
3. Jen Pollock Michel, *Teach Us to Want* (Downers Grove, IL: InterVarsity Press, 2014), 113.
4. Will Davis Jr., *The Power of Praying Boldly* (Grand Rapids, MI: Revell, 2007), 18.

Chapter 3: Dare to Pray With Endurance

1. Information from Warren Wiersbe, *The Wiersbe Bible Commentary* OT (Colorado Springs: David C. Cook, 2007), 495.
2. Ibid.

3. Jack Hayford, *New Spirit-Filled Life Bible* (Nashville: Thomas Nelson, 2002), 362, emphasis mine.

4. Samuel Chadwick, quoted in Adam Stadtmiller, *Praying for Your Elephant* (Colorado Springs: David C. Cook, 2015), 26.

5. Bruce Wilkinson, *Beyond Jabez* (Sisters, OR: Multnomah, 2005), 195.

Chapter 4: Dare to Pray and Say What's True

1. Strong's Interlinear Bible search on 2 Corinthians 4:13, StudyLight.org.

2. Lisa Whittle, *I Want God* (Eugene, OR: Harvest House, 2015), 22–23.

Chapter 5: Dare to Pray Like an Heir

1. My paraphrase of Warren Wiersbe, *The Wiersbe Bible Commentary NT* (Colorado Springs: David C. Cook, 2007).

2. NKJV *New Spirit-filled Life Bible* study note (Nashville: Thomas Nelson, 2002), 939.

Chapter 6: Dare to Pray Without Condemnation

1. Brennan Manning, *The Ragamuffin Gospel* (Sisters, OR: Multnomah, 2000), 39, 76, emphasis mine.

2. Warren Wiersbe, *The Wiersbe Bible Commentary NT* (Colorado Springs: David C. Cook, 2007), 476.

3. Patsy Clairmont, *You Are More Than You Know* (Brentwood, TN: Worthy Publishing, 2015), 47.

Chapter 7: Dare to Pray God's Promises

1. Radio interview with Adonis Lenzy, *Live the Promise with Susie Larson*, January 5, 2016.

2. In chapter 9 I address hindrances to our prayers and the importance of our obedience.

3. Jon Bloom, *Things Not Seen* (Wheaton, IL: Crossway, 2015), 128, emphasis mine.

4. Luke 7:22–23 NKJV

5. A.W. Tozer, *The Knowledge of the Holy* (New York: Harper & Row, 1961), 100.

Chapter 8: Dare to Pray From Victory

1. Chris Fabry, novelization of *War Room* (Carol Stream, IL: Tyndale House, 2015), 163.

2. Dudley Rutherford, *Walls Fall Down* (Nashville: Thomas Nelson, 2014), 25.

3. Max Lucado, *Glory Days* media promotional material (Nashville: Thomas Nelson, 2015).

4. Owen Strachan, *Risky Gospel* (Nashville: Thomas Nelson, 2013), 61, 23.

5. Bo Stern, *Ruthless* (Colorado Springs: NavPress, 2014), 63.

Chapter 9: Dare to Ask

1. A.W. Tozer, *Tozer for the Christian Leader* (Chicago: Moody Publishers, 2001), November 27 reading.

2. Andrew Murray, *Believing Prayer* (Minneapolis: Bethany House, 1980, 2004), 33–34, emphasis mine.

3. Mark Batterson, *The Circle Maker* (Grand Rapids, MI: Zondervan, 2011), 13.

4. Murray, *Believing Prayer*, 53–54, emphasis mine.

Chapter 10: Dare to Seek

1. A.W. Tozer, *I Talk Back to the Devil!* (Camp Hill, PA: Wing Spread Publishers, 1972, 1990), 15.

2. Excerpt from Kevin Gerald, *Good Things* (Colorado Springs: WaterBrook, 2015), accessed via YouVersion Bible devotional: "Believing God Is Good No Matter What."

3. Max Lucado, *Glory Days* (Nashville: Thomas Nelson, 2015), 124.

Chapter 11: Dare to Knock

1. Heather Holleman, *Seated With Christ* (Chicago: Moody Publishers, 2015), 93.

2. Curt Thompson, *The Soul of Shame* (Downers Grove, IL: IVP Books, 2015), 13, emphasis mine.

3. From Google Dictionary.

4. Mark Batterson, *Draw the Circle* (Grand Rapids, MI: Zondervan, 2012), 45.

Chapter 12: Dare to Dream

1. Will Davis Jr., *The Power of Praying Boldly* (Grand Rapids, MI: Revell, 2013), 28.

2. Kenneth Ulmer, *Knowing God's Voice* (Ventura, CA: Regal, 2011), 168.

Sample Prayers

1. Susie Larson, *The Uncommon Woman* (Chicago: Moody Publishers, 2008), 137–138.

Susie Larson is a popular author, national speaker, and radio host of her daily talk show, *Live the Promise with Susie Larson*. Susie has also served as a media voice for Moody Radio and was the former cohost for Focus on the Family's daily live talk show, *Everyday Relationships with Dr. Greg Smalley*. Her passion is to see women and men everywhere strengthened in their faith and mobilized to live out their high calling in Jesus Christ.

Her ten previous books include *Your Beautiful Purpose*, *Your Sacred Yes*, *Growing Grateful Kids*, *The Uncommon Woman*, *Blessings for the Evening*, and *Blessings for the Morning*.

Susie and her husband, Kevin, live near Minneapolis, Minnesota, and have three adult sons, two beautiful daughters-in-law, and one adorable pit bull. For more information, visit www.susielarson.com.

More From Susie Larson!

Visit SusieLarson.com to learn more.

In six 30-minute sessions, Susie Larson invites you to pray with reverence and expectation. Through personal stories and biblical insights, she will help you discover your unique identity in Christ and learn to pray more powerful prayers with faith and joy. Ideal for small group and church use.

Your Powerful Prayers DVD

Respond today to that nudge in your spirit—that desire to use your gifts and passions more fully in God's work—and discover God's beautiful purpose for your life.

Your Beautiful Purpose

It's so easy to give away our time to things un-appointed by God. In this practical and liberating book, Susie invites you to say no to overcommitment and yes to the life of joy, passion, and significance God has for you.

Your Sacred Yes

Blessings From Susie Larson

Visit SusieLarson.com to learn more.

Start your day with an uplifting reminder of God's promises, love, and purpose for you. Filled with biblical truth, these blessings offer strength and hope to help you face each new day.

Blessings for the Morning

Receive hope and encouragement at the end of every day with these nighttime blessings, which contain comforting reminders of God's peace, promises, and everlasting love.

Blessings for the Evening

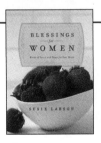

Nourish your heart with a reminder of God's love and purpose for you. Packed with biblical promise and perspective, these hope-filled blessings will bring joy to your soul.

Blessings for Women

◈BETHANYHOUSE